❄ **FROM THE FIRST DAY OF SCHOOL TO THE LAST** ❄

September

by Rebecca Stark

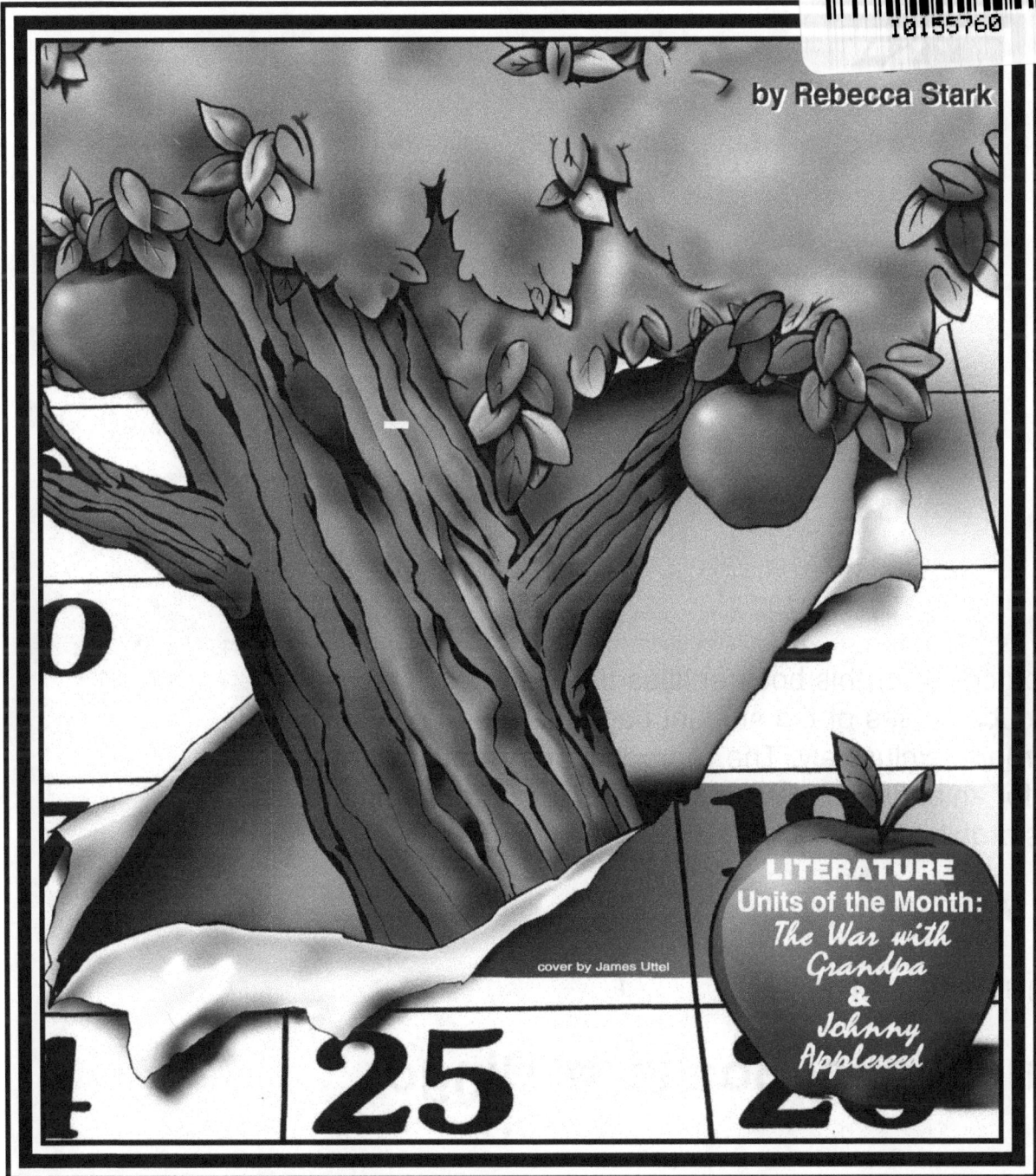

cover by James Uttel

LITERATURE
Units of the Month:
The War with Grandpa
&
Johnny Appleseed

Written by Rebecca Stark

ISBN 978-1-56644-607-5

Educational Books 'n' Bingo

Previously published by Educational Impressions, Inc.

Printed in the U.S.A.

Table of Contents

To the Teacher

Here's a month's worth of mind-stretching activities to help you make every day a special day. You'll find enrichment activities of varying levels of difficulty to tie in with events of the month. Adapt them to suit the needs of your students. Also included are mini-units, one or more literature units, creative writing ideas, clip art, and more. The crossword puzzle makes a great culminating activity for the month! All pages may be reproduced for use by the teacher for use in his or her classroom. Clip art may be enlarged or shrunken as suitable for your needs!

(Not Just) OPENERS FOR SEPTEMBER

Use these enrichment activities at the start of class, the end of class, as homework assignments, or any time you choose!

September 1

On September 1, 1865, Abraham Lincoln proposed the thirteenth amendment to the Constitution.

Find out the provisions of the thirteenth amendment.

September 2

Eugene Field was born September 2, 1850. He is known as the "Poet of Childhood."

Find out why.
Prepare an illustrated version of his most famous poem for a younger child.

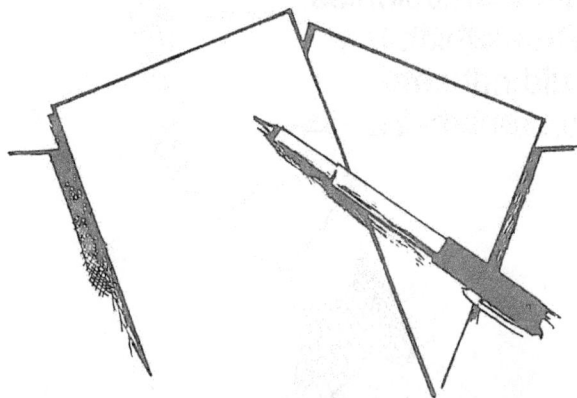

September 3

Louis Sullivan was born in Boston, Massachusetts, on September 3, 1856.

Draw a picture that illustrates his accomplishments.

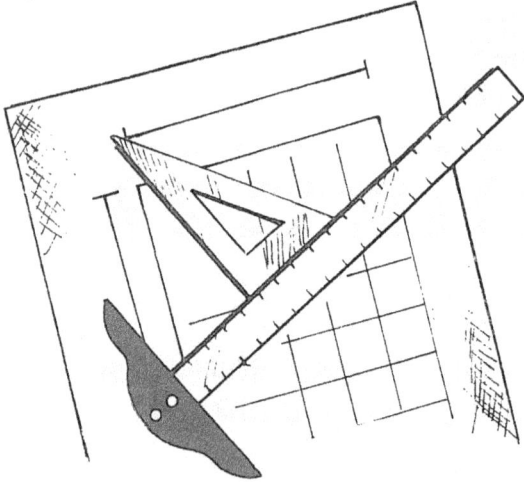

September 4

George Eastman received a patent on this day in 1888.

Write a letter to Mr. Eastman congratulating him for his invention and predicting its future importance.

September 5

The First Continental Congress met at Independence Hall in Philadelphia. Only one of the thirteen original colonies did not send representatives.

Draw a map of the thirteen colonies; show which one did not send representatives.

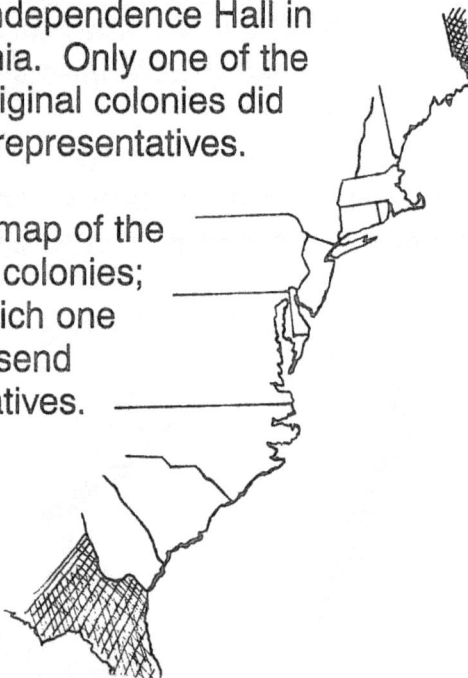

September 6

On September 6, 1901, President William McKinley was assassinated.

Find out where he was and why. Write his obituary.

6

September 7

Anna Mary Robertson, better known as Grandma Moses, was born on September 7, 1860.
She lived to be 101.

Write three questions you might have asked her on her 100th birthday. As Grandma Moses, answer those questions.

September 8

September 8th is International Literacy Day.

Create a poster to promote literacy in your hometown.

September 9

On September 9, 1965, Sandy Koufax pitched a perfect game for the L.A. Dodgers. No one reached first base.

Write a letter of congratulations.

September 10

On September 10, 1813, Oliver H. Perry defeated the British at the Battle of Lake Erie.

Explain the importance of this victory to the United States.

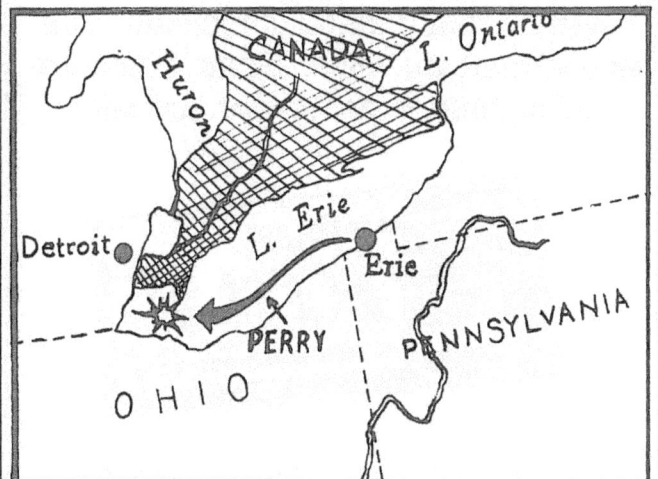

September 11

William Sidney Porter is better known by his pen name, O. Henry. He was born on September 11, 1862. His stories are known for their surprise endings.

Create the plot for a story with a surprise ending. Write a summary of the plot.

September 12

On September 12, 1940, four boys searching for a dog made a remarkable discovery in the caves of Lascaux, France.

Describe their find.

September 13

Milton Hershey was born on September 13, 1857. He spent years trying to perfect the chocolate bar! In 1903 he began building the world's largest chocolate manufacturing plant.

Create a poem about chocolate. Use any format you wish. Some ideas are haiku, shape poem, and acrostic.

MILK CHOCOLATE

September 14

William H. Armstrong, the author of *Sounder,* was born in Lexington, Virginia. *Sounder* tells the story of a sharecropper's family.

Write a paragraph explaining the term "sharecropper."

8

September 15

William Taft, the 27th President of the United States, was born on September 15, 1857. It was during his administration that the sixteenth amendment was passed.

Create a political cartoon using this amendment as the subject.

September 16

On this date in 1620 the Pilgrims left England on the *Mayflower*.

As a Pilgrim on that journey, write an entry in your diary.

September 17

On September 17, 1730, Frederich von Steuben was born.

As General George Washington, write a letter to Baron von Steuben thanking him for his assistance to the American cause. Be specific.

Thank You

September 18

Renowned African-American educator Booker T. Washington addressed the Atlanta Exposition on this date in 1895.

Write an encyclopedia entry for Booker T. Washington.

WASHINGTON BOOKER T.

9

September 19

On September 19, 1928, Mickey Mouse appeared for the first time in a black-and-white cartoon called *Steamboat Willie*.

See if you can find out what was special about that cartoon. Prepare three questions to ask Mickey Mouse about his debut.

September 20

Fiorello La Guardia, colorful mayor of New York City, died on September 20, 1947.

Research his life and write a eulogy for him.

September 21

French-Canadian fur trader, explorer, and cartographer Louis Jolliet was born on September 21, 1845.

Draw a map that shows the area he and Father Jacques Marquette explored.

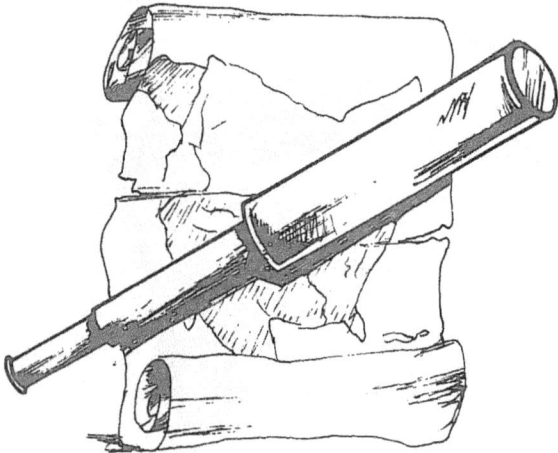

September 22

On September 22, 1961, the Peace Corps was established.

Create a recruitment poster to encourage people to join.

JOIN NOW

September 23

On September 23, 1779, Scottish-born naval hero John Paul Jones captured the British ship *Serapis* for the United States. During the early stages of the 3½-hour battle, the British asked him to surrender.

Find out his famous response.

September 24

Jim Henson was born on September 24, 1936. As the creator of the Muppets, Jim Henson revolutionized children's educational television.

In his honor, put on a puppet show that teaches a lesson to a young child.

September 25

Yosemite National Park was established on September 25, 1890.

Write a paragraph explaining why you do or do not think that national parks are important.

September 26

On September 26, 1820, Daniel Boone died. He helped blaze a trail through the Cumberland Gap.

Draw a map that includes the Wilderness Road. Assess the importance of that road.

11

September 27

On September 27, 1792, George Cruikshank was born. He was an artist, caricaturist, and illustrator. His most famous illustrations were for novelist Charles Dickens. He illustrated *Sketches by Boz* and *Oliver Twist*.

Define "caricature." In honor of George Cruikshank, draw a caricature of a well-known person.

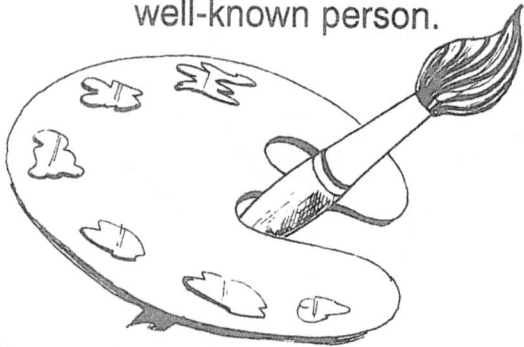

September 28

The birthday of Confucius is celebrated on September 28. His teachings were the base curriculum in China for more than 2,000 years!

Put the following excerpts from his teachings into your own words and tell whether or not you agree:
"The superior man is concerned with virtue; the inferior man is concerned with land."
"The superior man understands what is right; the inferior man understands what is profitable."

CONFUCIUS SAYS

September 29

Enrico Fermi was born on September 29, 1901.
This Italian Nobel Prize winner worked on the atomic bomb project at Los Alamos, NM.

Create a poster regarding the use of nuclear weapons.

ATOMIC BOMB

September 30

On September 30, 1927, baseball great Babe Ruth broke his own world record of 59 home runs in a season by hitting his 60th home run. This record stood until 1961.

Who beat Babe Ruth's record? Babe Ruth died in 1948. If he had been alive, how do you think he would have felt?

60th HOME RUN

Back-to-School Activities

Back to School

Think about all the things you did since the last day of school.
List ten things that you did.

1.

2.

3.

4.

5.

6.

7.

8.

9.

10.

Rate the things you just listed. Give the thing you enjoyed most a 10.
Give the thing you enjoyed least a 1.

Draw a picture of the thing you enjoyed most.

Hidden Back-to-School Words

The following back-to-school words are hiding in these sentences.
See if you can find them! The first one has been done for you.

> bookmark   bus   homework
> learn   paper   pen   play
> ruler   teacher   student

1. The job used to be Joe's.

2. "Grandpa, perhaps you'd like some ice cream," the child said.

3. Joe will bring one book. Mark will bring two.

4. In the zoo were one ape, nine monkeys, and two tigers.

5. I had tea; Cheryl had milk.

6. Follow this rule: running is not allowed.

7. Skip, lay the book on the table.

8. Stu dented the fender of his car.

9. Tammy came home, worked in the garden, and left.

10. Jill earns ten dollars an hour.

Scrambled Names

Create a scrambled name game. Choose ten classmates and scramble the letters in their names. You may use their first or last names.

Example:
ENJNIEFR=JENNIFER
ONJES=JONES

Exchange with classmates to solve.

What a Summer!

Compare this past summer to previous ones and to future ones.

How was this summer different from past summers?

_____

_____

_____

In what ways was this past summer better than previous ones?

_____

_____

_____

In what ways was this past summer worse than previous summers?

_____

_____

_____

How might future summers differ from this summer?

_____

_____

_____

Write a description of your perfect summer.

_____

_____

_____

_____

An Ideal Classroom

Add details to this picture to create an ideal classroom.

How does this ideal classroom differ from your classroom?

_____

_____

_____

_____

_____

What a Day!

You know how you feel on the first day of school,
but how does your teacher feel?
From your teacher's point of view, complete these entries in a diary.

Dear Diary,

   Tomorrow is the first day of school.

_____

_____

_____

_____

_____

_____

_____

Dear Diary,

   Today was the first day of school.

_____

_____

_____

_____

_____

_____

_____

Welcome

Have you ever had to change schools? If so, tell how you felt. If not, try to imagine how you might feel.

_____

_____

_____

List three things you might say or do to make new students feel welcome in your class.

_____

_____

_____

List three things a new student might say or do to become a part of the class.

_____

_____

_____

List three things your teacher might say or do to make a new student feel welcome.

_____

_____

_____

Classroom Rules

Do you think it is important to have rules? Explain.

_____

_____

List ten rules you think would be useful in a well-run classroom.

1. _____

2. _____

3. _____

4. _____

5. _____

6. _____

7. _____

8. _____

9. _____

10. _____

Now rate your rules in order of importance. Give the **most important rule the number 1** and the **least important one the number 10.**

21

Labor Day

Labor Day was first observed on September 5, 1882.
It was the idea of Peter J. McGuire, president of the
United Brotherhood of Carpenters and Joiners of America.
Today Labor Day is a legal holiday in the United States.

It is celebrated the first Monday in September.

People have many kinds of jobs. Stretch your imagination and classify these jobs into as many different groups as you can. You must have at least two in a group! Two groups have been started for you.

Example:
Work with food: Chef, Waiter
Two-word Jobs: Bus driver, Travel agent

mayor	gymnast	farmer
carpenter	chef	waiter
bus driver	cashier	artist
pilot	principal	director
teacher	astronaut	lawyer
doctor	police officer	homemaker
pediatrician	stockbroker	babysitter
veterinarian	banker	hotel manager
lion tamer	actor	tour guide
travel agent	baseball player	golfer
salesclerk	plumber	electrician
firefighter	taxi driver	computer operator
librarian	actress	senator

No Business Transacted!

In many places Labor Day has become a big shopping day. Do you think businesses should be closed on Labor Day?

Create a poster that expresses your opinion.

Sketch your idea here.

A Literature Unit

THE WAR WITH GRANDPA

by Robert Kimmel Smith

The first Sunday after Labor Day is **National Grandparents' Day.** In honor of Grandparents' Day, read *The War with Grandpa*, by Robert Kimmel Smith. It is the story of a boy who resents having to give up his room to his grandfather. Although he loves his grandfather dearly, he decides to declare war on him in order to regain his room.

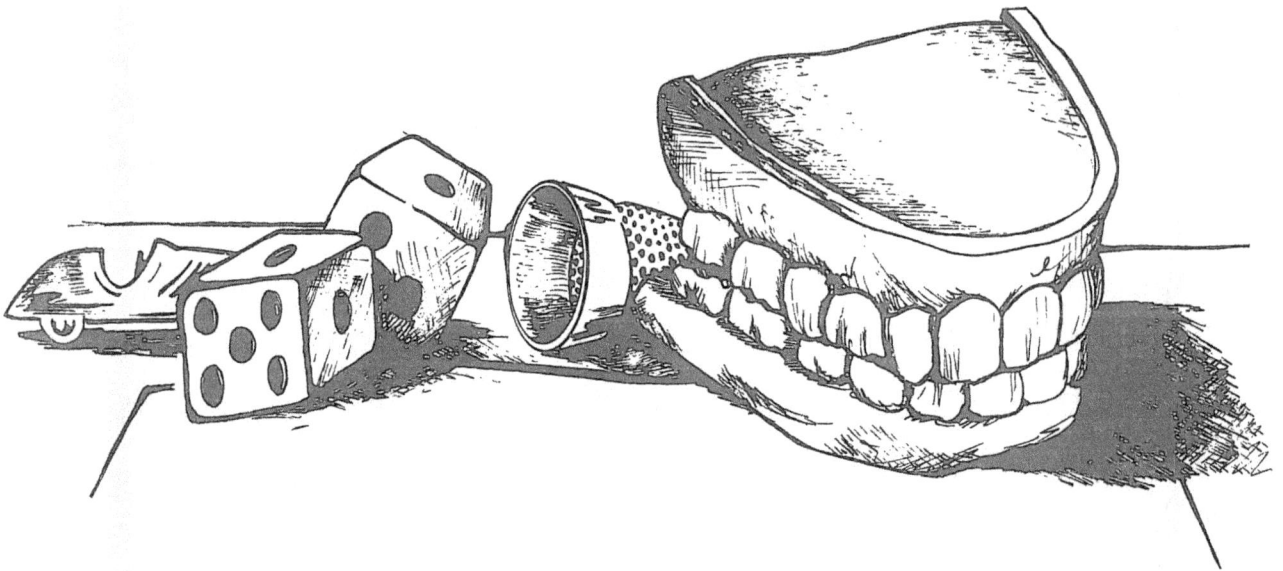

Chapters 1-5

Vocabulary: Match the vocabulary word on the left with the definition on the right.

___1. billboard   a. polite behavior
___2. ignore   b. of small size; insignificant
___3. pose   c. a structure for display of advertisements
___4. Venetian blind   d. to hold position, as in sitting for a portrait
___5. courtesy   e. to refuse to pay attention to
___6. dinky   f. window screen with horizontal slots

Comprehension & Discussion Questions

1. This book is written in the first person. Explain.

_____

_____

2. What did Pete mean when he said that Jennifer looked like a walking billboard?

_____

_____

3. What was Jennifer's secret? How did Jennifer learn it? In your opinion, did she keep the secret?

_____

_____

4. Summarize the reason Pete did not want to give up his room.

_____

_____

5. Judge Pete's reaction to his parents' insistence that he would have to move out of his room. How would you have felt?

_____

_____

Follow-up Activities

1. Describe your room. Tell what you do and do not like about it.
2. Use the saying "Life Isn't Always Fair" as the title for a short story.

Chapters 6-10

Vocabulary: Match the vocabulary word on the left with the definition on the right.

____1. ashamed	*a.* sad; dejected
____2. rickety	*b.* in ballet, a full turn on one's toes
____3. hunky-dory	*c.* feeling guilty
____4. crinkle	*d.* to drive or scare away
____5. pirouette	*e.* likely to break; shaky
____6. shoo	*f.* to form into wrinkles or ripples
____7. depressed	*g.* fine; quite satisfactory

Comprehension & Discussion Questions

1. In Chapter 6, Pete's promise changed from the original form. What does this tell us about Pete?

_____

_____

2. What is the main point of Chapter 8?

_____

_____

3. Compare Pete's reason that he loved his grandparents to Jenny's reason for loving her grandfather, given in chapter 4.

_____

_____

4. Why did Pete's grandparents move to Florida?

_____

_____

5. Why was Mom upset?

_____

_____

Follow-up Activities

1. Make a list of what you won't allow your kids to do.

2. Pete collects baseball cards. Write a paragraph about a hobby you have or would like to have.

Chapters 11-16

Vocabulary: Match the vocabulary word on the left with the definition on the right.

___ 1. mope   a. a person with an excessive interest in something
___ 2. invade   b. a formal statement or announcement
___ 3. fanatic   c. to give oneself up to brooding and sulking
___ 4. formation   d. a plan of action
___ 5. scout   e. a specific arrangement, as in troops
___ 6. declaration   f. to enter by force in order to conquer
___ 7. strategy   g. to search

Comprehension & Discussion Questions

1. Compare Grandpa before and after Grandma's illness.

_____

_____

2. Did you ever hear the expression "to egg someone on"? Use that expression to explain what happened in Chapter 12.

_____

_____

3. Judge Pete's Declaration of War. Did it clearly state what he wanted and why?

_____

_____

4. Do you think Grandpa saw the note? Why or why not?

_____

_____

5. Propose a reason Grandpa might have acted as if he hadn't read the note.

_____

_____

Follow-up Activities

1. Suppose Pete had asked you for help in composing a Declaration of War. Compile a list of demands and explanations Pete could have written.
2. Think of something you believe is unfair. Compile your own Declaration of War.

Chapter 17-21

Vocabulary: Match the vocabulary word on the left with the definition on the right.

___1. digital   a. a temporary stopping of hostilities
___2. surrender   b. fighting by small, independent groups
___3. fumble   c. using or giving a reading in number symbols
___4. truce   d. making known something previously unknown
___5. guerrilla warfare   e. to give up possession of something
___6. revealing   f. to mishandle

Comprehension & Discussion Questions

1. How would you have reacted to being awakened at 3:00 A.M. if you had been Grandpa?

_____

_____

2. Explain what is meant by a flag of truce.

_____

_____

3. Do you agree that Pete was spoiled? Explain.

_____

_____

4. Pete used a pun in the note he left when he stole the slippers. Grandpa also used a pun when he found them. Explain.

_____

_____

5. Why, do you think, did Pete get annoyed at Grandpa's reaction to his statement that this was guerrilla warfare?

_____

_____

Follow-up Activities

1. A pun is a play on words. Sometimes it uses different senses of the same word. Sometimes it makes a play on the similar sense or sound of different words. Create your own pun.
2. Choose sides. Explain why you have chosen Pete's or Grandpa's side.

Chapters 22-25

Vocabulary: Match the vocabulary word on the left with the definition on the right.

___1. meander   a. a deep-seated feeling of resentment
___2. grudge   b. pertaining to the sense of smell
___3. obnoxious   c. to wander idly without fixed direction
___4. campaign   d. unquestionably
___5. olfactory   e. very disagreeable or offensive
___6. indubitably   f. an operation undertaken by means of propaganda to attain a goal

Comprehension & Discussion Questions

1. Judge Grandpa's statement: "The only time you have to fight a war is when someone attacks you. Then, and only then, you have the right to defend yourself."

_____

_____

2. Guess why Grandpa slapped Pete.

_____

_____

3. Pete used a simile to describe Jenny as she was dancing. Explain.

_____

_____

4. How did Grandpa retaliate for Pete's tricks?

_____

_____

5. According to Steve, why was it good that Grandpa stole the game pieces?

_____

_____

Follow-up Activities

1. In Chapter 23 we learned how Jenny got what she wanted. Describe how you go about getting what you want. Is it effective?

2. Pete's friends tried to get him to do things he shouldn't. Have your friends ever used peer pressure to get you to do something? Did they succeed? Explain.

Chapters 26-28

Vocabulary: Match the vocabulary word on the left with the definition on the right.

___1. peg
___2. asterisk
___3. tide
___4. gravitation
___5. footloose
___6. play hardball

a. the natural of attraction between massive bodies
b. free to do as one pleases
c. a star-shaped figure used as a reference
d. a small wooden pin used to fasten things
e. the variation in the surface level of the oceans
f. to use any means, however ruthless, to obtain an objective

Comprehension & Discussion Questions

1. Grandpa used a metaphor in explaining why he wouldn't return the Monopoly pieces. Explain.

_____

_____

2. The war between Pete and Grandpa had a beneficial effect on Grandpa. Explain.

_____

_____

3. Why did Grandpa want to leave early to go fishing?

_____

_____

4. Pete responded humorously to Grandpa's explanation about the importance of the tides. Explain.

_____

_____

5. What was the next trick that Pete played on Grandpa? Why?

_____

_____

Follow-up Activities

1. Draw a chart that illustrates the moon's effect upon the oceans.
2. Pete's first fishing experience was memorable. Write about a "favorite first" you experienced. A few ideas are the first time you went camping, the first time you rode a bike, the first time you flew on a plane, and the first time you went to a wedding.

Chapters 29-32

Vocabulary: Match the vocabulary word on the left with the definition on the right.

____1. diabolical   a. a large mouthful
____2. psychological warfare   b. paying back evil for evil
____3. retrieve   c. wicked; appropriate to a devil
____4. revenge   d. the use of tactics that influence the mind or emotions
____5. gulp   e. a meeting for consultation or discussion
____6. conference   f. to get back; to regain
____7. retaliation   g. to inflict punishment in return for an injury or insult

Comprehension & Discussion Questions

1. Explain the expression "waiting for the other shoe to drop" in the context of this story.

_____

_____

2. Why, do you think, did Grandpa return the Monopoly pieces?

_____

_____

3. How did Grandpa finally get his revenge for the watch?

_____

_____

4. Why did Pete have to "beg" lunch?

_____

_____

5. What lesson did Pete finally learn?

_____

_____

Follow-up Activities

1. Plan a treasure hunt. Tell what will be hidden and where you will hide each item. Will your treasure hunt have a theme?
2. Devise a trick that Pete might pull on Grandpa to end this war once and for all.

Chapters 33-37

Vocabulary: Match the vocabulary word on the left with the definition on the right.

_____ 1. translate   a. a wall (or section) made up of flat, rectangular pieces
_____ 2. bunk   b. a booth or cubical
_____ 3. duct   c. to work at a job in addition to your regular job
_____ 4. paneling   d. to sleep, especially in makeshift quarters
_____ 5. privacy   e. to express in another language
_____ 6. stall   f. the condition of being secluded from others
_____ 7. moonlight   g. a tubular passage through which a substance is conveyed

Comprehension & Discussion Questions

1. Judge Pete's actions. Was it funny or cruel to steal Grandpa's teeth?

_____

_____

2. Why, do you think, did Pete return the teeth?

_____

_____

3. What important lesson about war did Pete learn?

_____

_____

4. How did Pete and Grandpa resolve their problem?

_____

_____

5. What important lesson did Pete learn about peer pressure?

_____

_____

Follow-up Activities

1. If your teacher asked you to write a story about something important that happened to you, what would you write about? Make an outline for your story.

2. Judge the way Pete's parents handled Grandpa's move into their home. Would you have done something different? Write a letter to them giving your point of view.

An Acrostic

An **acrostic** is a poem that uses the letters of the subject as the first letter of each line. The lines may consist of a word or two or they may be complete sentences. They do not have to rhyme.

Write an acrostic poem about grandparents in general or about your grandparents in particular. Some possible titles are Grandma, Grandpa, Grandmothers, Grandfathers, Gramps, and Grammy. If you prefer, use the name you call your grandmother or grandfather: Grammy Anna, Papa John, or whatever name you use.

G
R
A
N
D
M
A

G
R
A
N
D
P
A

Breakfast Food
Word Search

September is Better Breakfast Month.
List as many different breakfast foods and beverages as you can.

Use your list of words to create a word-search puzzle!

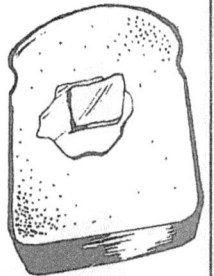

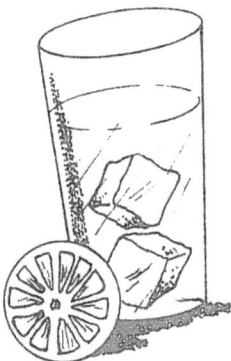

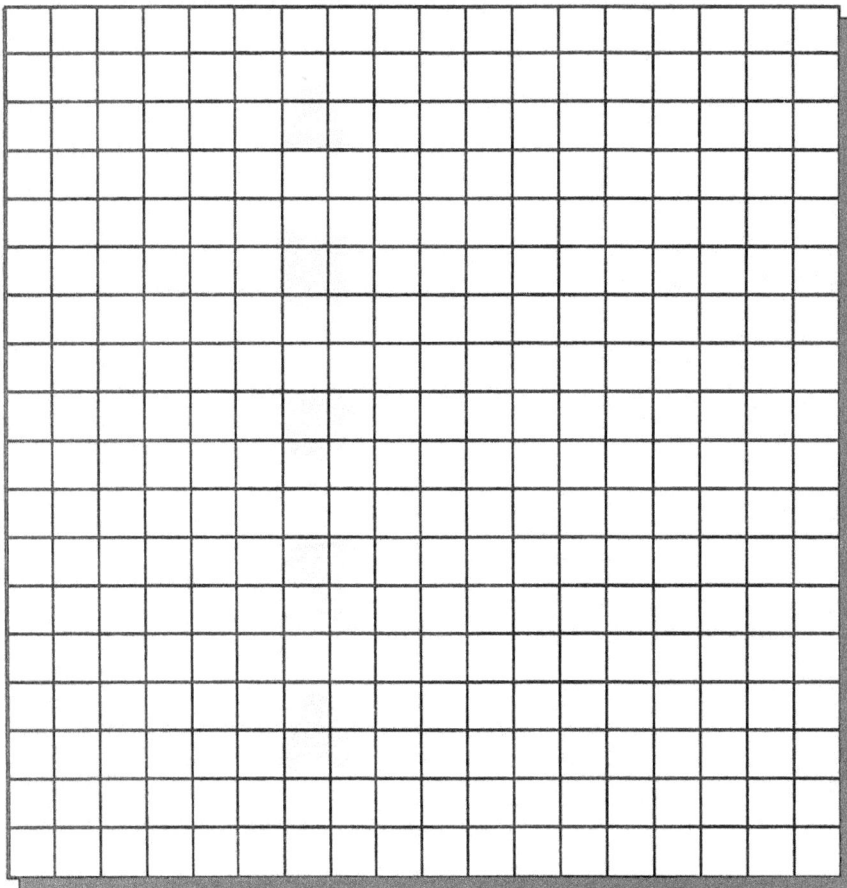

Exchange with a classmate to solve!

A Great Way to Start the Day

Pretend you have just opened a new restaurant.
Your restaurant specializes in breakfast.

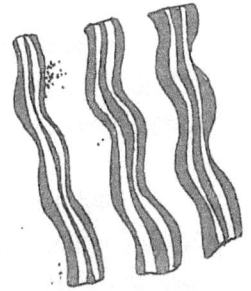

Create four specials.
Each should be both healthy and appealing.
Name your specials.

Special #1

Special #2

Special #3

Special #4

Lafayette: A French-American Hero

Marie-Joseph-Paul-Yves-Roch-Gilbert du Motier, Marquis de Lafayette, was born on September 6, 1757. It was a long name for a little boy, but Gilbert, as he was called, would live up to that name!

When the American Revolution began, the young Marquis de Lafayette was very much taken with the American cause. At the time, he was captain of a regiment encamped on the eastern border of France. He tried to get leave so he could go to America, but he could not. Without telling even his young wife, he bought a ship and with some volunteers he sailed for America.

At first, Congress refused his help. They thought that he and his men were just seeking adventure. But when they realized that he wanted no pay and that he came from a wealthy, influential family, they changed their minds. By the time he was twenty, Lafayette would find himself in command of the Virginia troops!

Lafayette was greatly admired by General Washington and his troops. He did a great deal to help the Americans. One way he helped was with his successful mission to the Iroquois. The Iroquois had been helping the British. After having been made an honorary member of the tribe, Lafayette returned with 50 Iroquois willing to help the Americans.

Another way Lafayette helped was by urging his fellow countrymen to support the American cause. He wrote letter after letter and was pleased when he learned that a Treaty of Friendship between France and America was passed and that some ships would be sent to help. But he knew this wouldn't be enough. Lafayette returned to France. He convinced the king of France that it was in the best interest of France to help the Americans defeat the English. General Washington was gratified when Lafayette sent word that more guns, supplies, and ships would follow!

After a delay caused by the English blockade of the French harbor, news finally arrived that French warships were on their way to Yorktown, Virginia. General Washington attacked the British at Yorktown by land. The French ships prevented the British from getting help! The British were forced to surrender. The war was not over, but this American victory at Yorktown—a victory due in part to the persistence of the Marquis de Lafayette—brought the war close to an end.

A Family Motto

On the Lafayettes' coat of arms was the motto
"CUR NON?" It means **"WHY NOT?"** in Latin.

From what you know about the Marquis de Lafayette,
do you think his family motto was appropriate for him? Explain.

_____

_____

_____

_____

_____

Think about your family. **Stretch your imagination** and
try to think of some possible mottoes.

Choose the motto you like best and write it on this shield.

_____

_____

_____

_____

_____

_____

_____

_____

_____

37

An Epitaph

An epitaph is an inscription written on a
tombstone in honor of the person buried there.

Create an epitaph for the Marquis de Lafayette.

MARQUIS DE LAFAYETTE

Jane Addams:
Founder of Hull-House

Jane Addams was born to a well-to-do, respected family on September 6, 1860, and was raised in Cedarville, Ohio. Jane was well educated and even attended Woman's Medical College in Philadelphia. Ill health caused her to leave before she finished her medical studies.

While traveling in Europe, Jane saw many disturbing sights. In London and other cities, she was shocked by the poverty and wretchedness of the slums. She soon realized, however, that similar conditions existed in America as well. She became determined to do something about it!

It was in Chicago that Jane decided to make her dream a reality. Jane Addams founded Hull-House on September 18, 1889. She resolved that Hull-House would be open to all creeds, races, and nationalities. Helping her was her good friend Ellen Starr. At first people were leery about the wealthy "do-gooder." Soon, however, they came to understand that they were truly welcome at Hull House.

Hull-House became a place where those in need could turn when they needed a meal. But Hull-House provided much more than food. There were programs for both adults and children. These programs included classes in painting, handicrafts, and music as well as lectures in science and the humanities.

Jane Addams did more for social reform than run Hull-House. She was an advocate for children's rights and lectured against sweatshops that exploited little girls. She was also a staunch ally of the suffragettes and helped women in Chicago get the right to vote. Jane was interested in the rights of all people; in 1910 she helped found the National Association for the Advancement of Colored People (NAACP).

Jane Addams was a pacifist; she did not believe in war as a means of settling disputes. Even so, when the United States entered World War I in 1917, she turned her energies toward helping those victimized by the war. When President Hoover asked for volunteers, Jane signed on to work for the Food Administration. In November 1931, Jane Addams was awarded the Nobel Peace Prize. She donated most of the money to the Women's International League of Peace and Freedom.

After devoting her life to those in need, Jane Addams died on May 21, 1935.

Chicago

Research conditions in Chicago in the latter quarter of the nineteenth century. Decide whether or not it was a suitable location for the challenge of the establishment of a social settlement.

List at least five facts to support your opinion.

_____

_____

_____

_____

_____

_____

Please Don't Do It

Jane's stepmother, Anna, was very embarrassed by Jane's decision to found Hull-House. She didn't think that a refined girl with her background should choose to live in the slums of a frightening city.

As Anna, write a letter to Jane describing how you feel.

Dear Jane,

_____

_____

_____

_____

_____

_____

_____

As Jane, explain why you will not change your course of action.

Dear Stepmother,

_____

_____

_____

_____

_____

_____

_____

Grandma Moses:
It's Never Too Late

Anna Mary Robertson was born in Greenwich, New York, on September 7, 1860. Even as a child, Anna Mary loved to paint. She and the other children collected berries and used their juices to paint. Her mother did little to encourage Anna Mary; she believed she'd be better off spending her time doing more practical work.

When Anna Mary was twelve, she had to leave school to go to work. She got a job as a housekeeper for a wealthy family; Anna Mary remained with them for four years before moving to a new family. Her new mistress encouraged her to return to school, which she did.

When Anna Mary was twenty-seven, she married Thomas Salmon Moses. The two headed for North Carolina. On the way they stopped in Stauton, Virginia; they remained there as dairy farmers for eighteen years before returning to New York State.

Anna Mary would have loved to spend her time painting, but she had little time to spare. In addition to her farm work, she had five children to raise! It wasn't until all her children had married that Anna Mary started to paint again!

And it wasn't until she was seventy-eight years old that people really started to notice her paintings. Her youngest son Hugh and his wife had arranged to have some of her work put on display in the local drug store. An art collector bought all the paintings she had. A year later the collector told her that three of her works would be on display in the Museum of Modern Art in New York. She was seventy-nine years old!

Anna Mary Moses still remained virtually unknown. Finally, an art dealer agreed to show some of her paintings in his gallery. It was in an article that appeared in the New York *Herald Tribune* that the name Grandma Moses first appeared. The headline read as follows: "Grandma Moses, untaught upstate artist, to show works at city gallery." The name stuck!

As Grandma Moses's paintings got more exposure, more and more people grew to love her work. They were fascinated by the fact that she managed to start a successful new career when she was almost eighty years old. She was a great motivation for many!

Grandma Moses died on December 13, 1961.

Who Was President?

Grandma Moses lived from September 7, 1860, to December 13, 1961. Make a chart that shows all the people who served as President of the United States during her lifetime.

President   From   To

EXTRA:

Find out what **tragic event** took place on **April 14, 1865,** when Anna Mary was 4¹/₂ years old? What **tragic event** took place in the **summer of 1881?**

_____

_____

43

Happy Birthday!

In honor of Grandma Moses's birthday, create a poem about her. Your poem should honor some of the qualities you admire about her.

Fact or Opinion

A fact is a statement that can be proven.   An opinion may be defined as a personal belief. Read each statement below. Decide if it is a fact or an opinion and place an "F" or an "O" in the space provided.

Examples:
> *Fact:* Ice cream is made from cream, sugar, and flavoring.
> *Opinion:* Chocolate ice cream is more delicious than vanilla.

_____ 1. Anna Mary Robertson was born on September 7, 1860.

_____ 2. Anna Mary first became famous in her eighties.

_____ 3. Grandma Moses was Anna Mary's nickname.

_____ 4. Grandma Moses was a talented artist.

_____ 5. Eighty years of age is too old to start painting.

_____ 6. Everyone should have a hobby.

_____ 7. Grandma Moses won several awards.

_____ 8. Grandma Moses deserved the awards.

_____ 9. Anna Mary and Thomas Moses were dairy farmers.

_____ 10. Painting is more worthwhile than dairy farming.

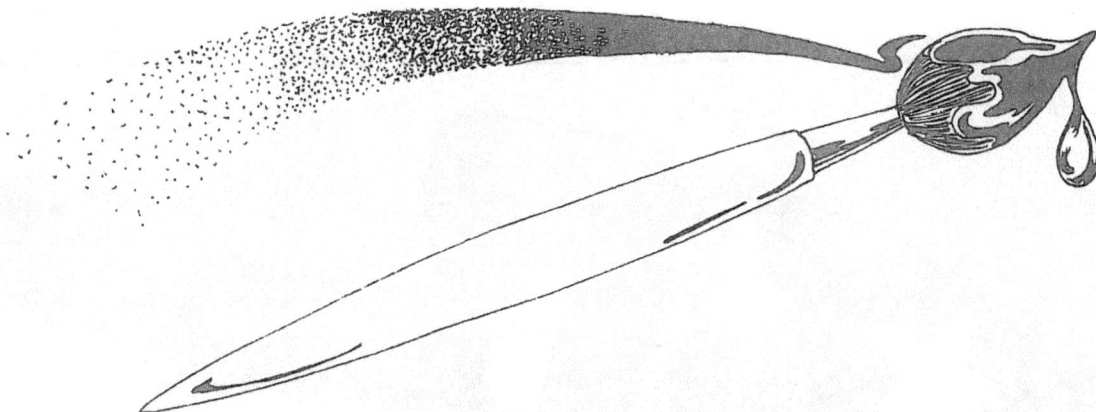

The Pledge of Allegiance

The *Pledge of Allegiance* was first published on September 8, 1892. Substitute your own words for those words printed in bold.

I **pledge allegiance** to the flag of the United States of America and to the **republic** for which it **stands**. One nation, under God, **indivisible**, with **liberty**, and **justice** for all.

pledge:
allegiance:
republic:
stands:
indivisible:
liberty:
justice:

Now rewrite the *Pledge of Allegiance* in your own words.

_____

_____

_____

_____

_____

_____

_____

Jesse Owens

Jesse Owens was born on September 12, 1913, in Danville, Alabama. He was one of the greatest track-and-field athletes of all times. In 1936, Jesse Owens won four gold medals at the Olympics Games in Berlin, Germany. Adolf Hitler, the Nazi dictator of Germany, was very upset. Hitler believed that whites were better than blacks. Adolf Hitler refused to congratulate him. Instead, he walked out of the stadium! Jesse Owens died in 1980.

Write an **acrostic poem** about Jesse Owens.

J
E
S
S
E

O
W
E
N
S

Unlikely Correspondents

Not all Germans shared Adolf Hitler's views of Aryan supremacy. One who didn't share his views was Luz Long, Jesse's main competitor in the broad jump. In fact, it was Luz who gave Jesse some important hints about qualifying. In return, Jesse helped Luz apply liniment to his sore leg so that he could continue to jump. The two even wrote letters to each other until Luz was killed in the war.

Create a possible conversation between Jesse Owens and Luz Long after Adolf Hitler refused to shake Jesse's hand.

Luz: _____

_____

_____

Jesse: _____

_____

_____

Luz: _____

_____

_____

Jesse: _____

_____

_____

Luz: _____

_____

Jesse: _____

_____

_____

48

The Star-Spangled Banner

Francis Scott Key was a member of a prominent Maryland family. A few months after Congress declared war against England in 1812, Francis joined the army. It is not as a soldier, however, that we best remember Francis Scott Key; it is as the author of the United States national anthem.

The War of 1812, so named for the year it began, continued. On August 24, 1814, the British burned Washington. Many important buildings, including the President's Mansion, the Capitol, and the Library of Congress were destroyed. Francis Scott Key could see the fire that lit the skies from his home in nearby Georgetown.

When Key learned that his friend Dr. Beanes had been taken prisoner aboard an English ship, he got permission from President Madison to try to rescue him. With the government agent for prisoners, he sailed the flag of peace. The British agreed to let Dr. Beanes go in a few days. To his dismay, however, Key learned that the British planned to capture Baltimore in the meantime.

From the ship where they were held, Key could see Fort McHenry, which guarded the entrance to Baltimore Harbor. He watched as the British fleet approached the fort.

The battle on land was fought on September 12. By the next day, British warships had formed two half circles around the fort. The bombing of Fort McHenry had begun.

Through the day and the night Key watched the battle from the ship. He kept his field glasses focused on the flag. He knew that as long as the American flag flew over the fort all would be well. But in the morning mist he could see no flag. Which would it be? When the sky finally cleared, Key saw the stars and stripes and breathed a sigh of relief.

Francis Scott Key had always shown an aptitude for poetry. It was no surprise that on this momentous occasion he set his thoughts to poetry. He began to write as he watched the British ships withdraw from the harbor. He finished it later that night in Baltimore.

Francis Scott Key's poem was printed in *The Baltimore American*. It was entitled *The Defense of Fort McHenry*. Soon it was set to the tune of a popular old song, *To Anacreon in Heaven*. Before long, people in every state were singing the song written by the gentleman from Maryland. It became known as *The Star-Spangled Banner*.

In the 1890s *The Star-Spangled Banner* was made the official song of the U.S. Army and Navy. It was officially declared the national anthem of the United States in 1931.

The Star-Spangled Banner

Fill in the missing words.

O say can you see, by the _____ early light,
What so _____ we hail'd at the
_____ last gleaming,
Whose broad _____ and bright stars
through the perilous fight
O'er the _____ we watch'd
were so gallantly _____?

And the _____ red glare, the _____
bursting in air,
Gave _____ through the night that
our flag was still there.
O say does that star-spangled
banner yet _____
O'er the the land of the _____ and
the home of the _____?

A Shape Poem

A shape poem, sometimes called a concrete poem, is written in the shape of the thing it describes. It does not have to rhyme.
Here are two examples of shape poems. They were taken from *Take A Bite Out of Rhyme*, written by Cindi Nolen Allen and published by Educational Impressions.

Pickle. Green, crunchy, juicy, sliced, whole, sour

PICKLE

KISS

A silvery wrapper holds this chocolate treat for me to eat.

Now write a shape poem about the flag. List many different words that describe the flag. Include words that tell how you feel about it.

_____ _____ _____

_____ _____ _____

_____ _____ _____

_____ _____ _____

Use your list to help you create a shape poem about the flag.

A Letter Home

Suppose Francis Scott Key had not been inclined to write poetry.
What if he had written a letter home to his wife, Polly, instead?
As Francis, write a letter to Polly describing your thoughts and
feelings before, during, and after the attack on Fort McHenry.

Dear Polly,

_____

_____

_____

_____

_____

_____

_____

_____

_____

_____

_____

_____

_____

_____

_____

_____

_____

_____

Second Choice

Suppose Francis Scott Key had not written *The Star-Spangled Banner*.
What song might have been chosen to be America's national anthem?
Brainstorm all the songs that might have been considered.

_____

_____

_____

_____

_____

Which of the songs is best suited to be the anthem? Explain.

_____

_____

_____

_____

_____

Compare the song you have chosen to *The Star-Spangled Banner*.
In what ways is each better suited to be the
national anthem of the United States?

_____

_____

_____

_____

_____

Old People's Day

Old People's Day, or Respect for the Aged Day,
is a national holiday in Japan. It is held on September 15.

What age do you think of as old?_____

_____

Do you have grandparents? Are they old? _____

_____

Think about an old person you know.
What nice things could you do for that person?

_____

_____

_____

_____

_____

_____

_____

_____

_____

_____

_____

_____

_____

Agatha Christie

Agatha Christie was born on September 15, 1890, in England. She began writing detective stories while a nurse during World War I. Her first novel was published in 1920. It was in that novel that she first introduced Hercule Poirot; she included this eccentric Belgian detective in about 25 novels. Another popular detective character used in several of her novels was the elderly Miss Jane Marple.

Create-a-Mystery

Use this outline to help you create a mystery.

YOUR DETECTIVE

Name: _____ Sex: _____ Age: _____

Physical Description: _____

_____

Personality: _____

_____

Educational Background: _____

_____

Occupation, if any, other than detective: _____

Strengths and weaknesses: _____

_____

PLOT

Who?: _____

_____

What?: _____

_____

Where?: _____

_____

When?: _____

_____

Why?: _____

_____

How?: _____

_____

Remember, your story must have a beginning, where you introduce your readers to the characters and the situation; a middle, where you develop the plot; and an ending where all the situations are resolved.

Write your mystery on other paper.

Hispanic Heritage Week

The second Sunday in September begins Hispanic Heritage Week. In honor of Hispanic Heritage Week, match each person on the left with the appropriate description on the right.

___ 1. Joan Baez   A. Mexican-American labor leader

___ 2. Simón Bolívar   B. President of Argentina

___ 3. Pablo Casals   C. Spanish philosopher and poet

___ 4. Caesar Chavez   D. Puerto Rican baseball player

___ 5. Henry Cisneros   E. Spanish artist

___ 6. Roberto Clemente   F. Mexican-American H.U.D. Secretary

___ 7. Hernán Cortés   G. Spanish cellist

___ 8. Jaime Escalante   H. Mexican-American folksinger

___ 9. Gloria Estefan   I. Mexican-American educator

___ 10. Andy Garcia   J. Mexican revolutionary

___ 11. Pablo Neruda   K. Spanish explorer

___ 12. Evita Perón   L. Cuban-American movie star

___ 13. Juan Perón   M. Cuban-American singer

___ 14. Pablo Picasso   N. Chilean poet

___ 15. George Santayana   O. Latin-American revolutionary

___ 16. Pancho Villa   P. First lady of Argentina

Hispanic Heritage Week

The following people of Hispanic heritage were listed in the previous matching activities: Joan Baez, Simón Bolívar, Pablo Casals, Caesar Chavez, Henry Cisneros, Roberto Clemente, Hernán Cortés, Jaime Escalante, Gloria Estefan, Andy Garcia, Pablo Neruda, Evita Perón, Juan Perón, Pablo Picasso, George Santayana, and Pancho Villa.

Use these people as the basis for the activities on this page.

Choose ten people and scramble their names. Exchange with your classmates to solve.

Create a Hispanic heritage word search. Exchange with your classmates to solve.

Choose five people. Research and write five facts about each.

Choose one of these people and write an acrostic poem.

Create three "Who am I?" riddles. Exchange with your classmates to solve.

Take turns role playing one of these people. Have the others try to guess who is being imitated.

58

Hablo Español

Hablo Español means "I speak Spanish." The following are some countries in which Spanish is spoken. Unscramble the letters to find out what they are.

1. EMIXOC

   _____

2. UCAB

   _____

3. OTREUP OCIR

   _____

4. PAINS

   _____

5. ONHDURSA

   _____

6. RAGENANIT

   _____

7. LCOMIOBA

   _____

8. UREP

   _____

9. OCSTA RCIA

   _____

10. AUGARACIN

    _____

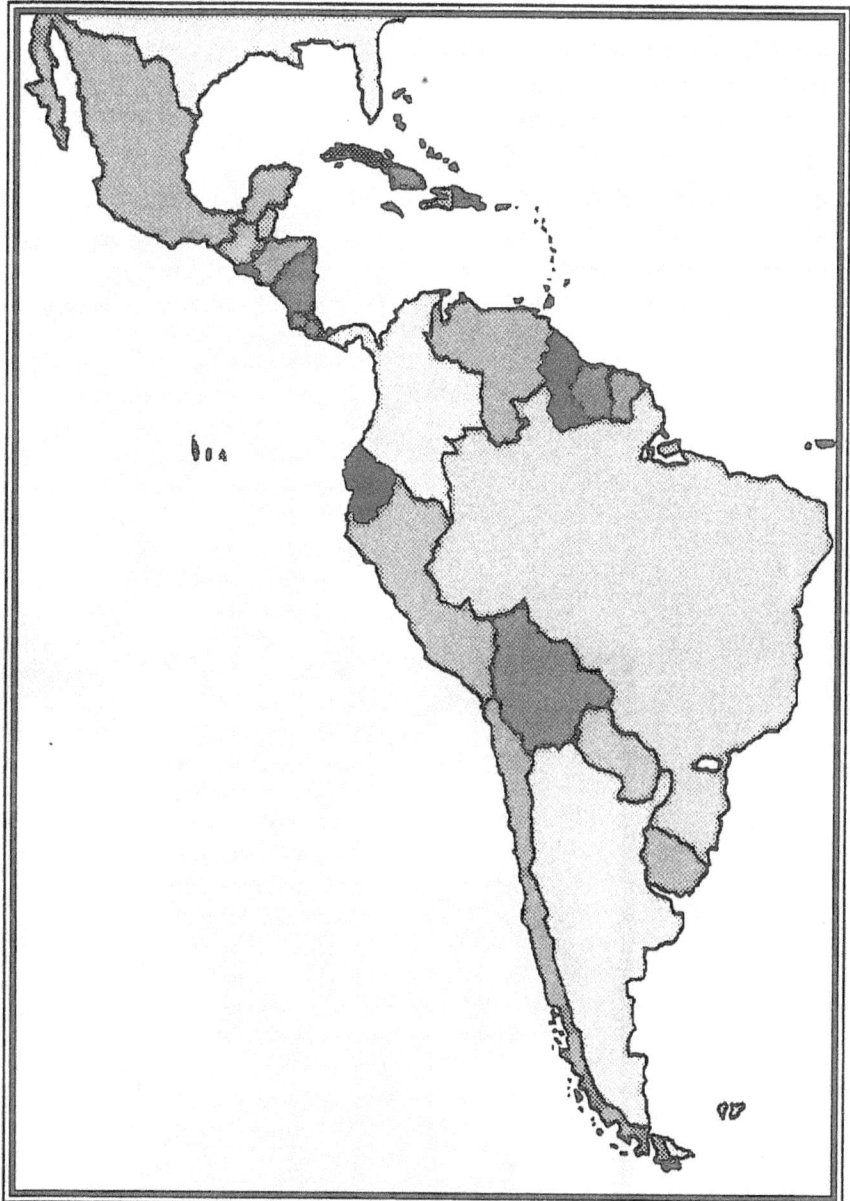

MEXICAN INDEPENDENCE DAY

September 16 is **Mexican Independence Day.** It celebrates the day in 1810 when a priest named Miguel Hidalgo called the people of Dolores together and asked them to fight for their independence from Spain. His plea became known as *El Grito de Dolores,* or *"the cry from Dolores."* His *grito* inspired the revolution, but Hidalgo did not live to see independence achieved. He was captured by Spanish soldiers in 1811 and shot as a traitor. To the Mexican people, however, Father Hidalgo was a hero. He became known as the Father of the Mexican Revolution. Mexico finally won its independence from Spain in 1821.

A Mexican Vacation

Pretend that you are a travel agent. Your clients want to spend a few weeks in Mexico. Plan a detailed itinerary for them. Choose from the following locations or add your own recommendations:
Mexico City, Acapulco, Cancún, Cozumel, Puerto Vallarta, Taxco, Tulúm, and Xochimilco.

Use the following questions to help plan the trip.

How would your clients travel to and from Mexico?

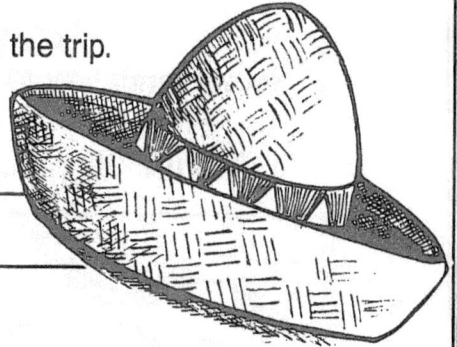

_____

_____

Which locations would your clients visit?

_____

_____

How much time would be spent in each place?

_____

_____

What sights would be visited in each place?

_____

_____

What side trips would be made from each place?

_____

_____

What sports or other activities will be offered at each place?

_____

_____

¿Cuántos Dólares?
How many dollars?

At the writing of this book the Mexican peso was worth **.133 dollars**. The U.S. dollar was worth **7.50 pesos**.

Suppose you were traveling in Mexico.
How much would you pay in U.S. dollars for each item below?

1. **T-shirt** 50 pesos

2. **Soda** 6 pesos

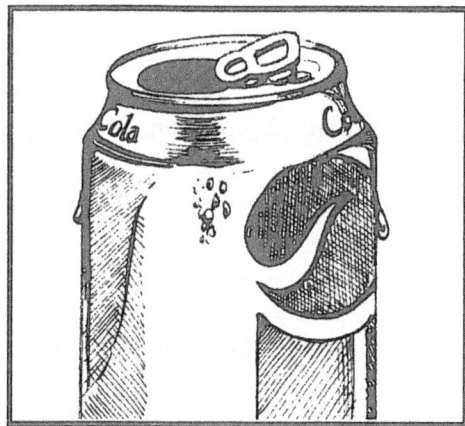

3. **Sandwich** 35 pesos

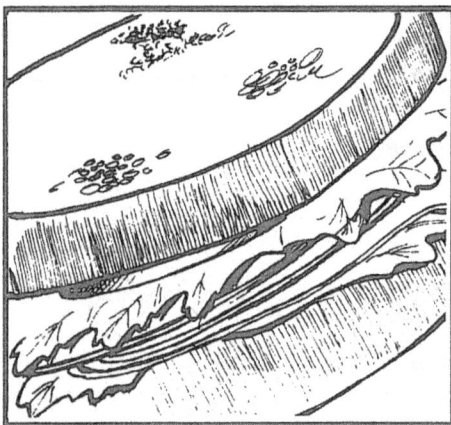

4. **Dress** 250 pesos

Mexico

1. Fill in the borders.

2. Add the following cities: **Mexico City, Xochimilco, Taxco, Acapulco, Puerto Vallarta, Cancún, Tulúm, and Cozumel.**

3. Indicate which is the capital.

4. Add any landmarks or features you wish.

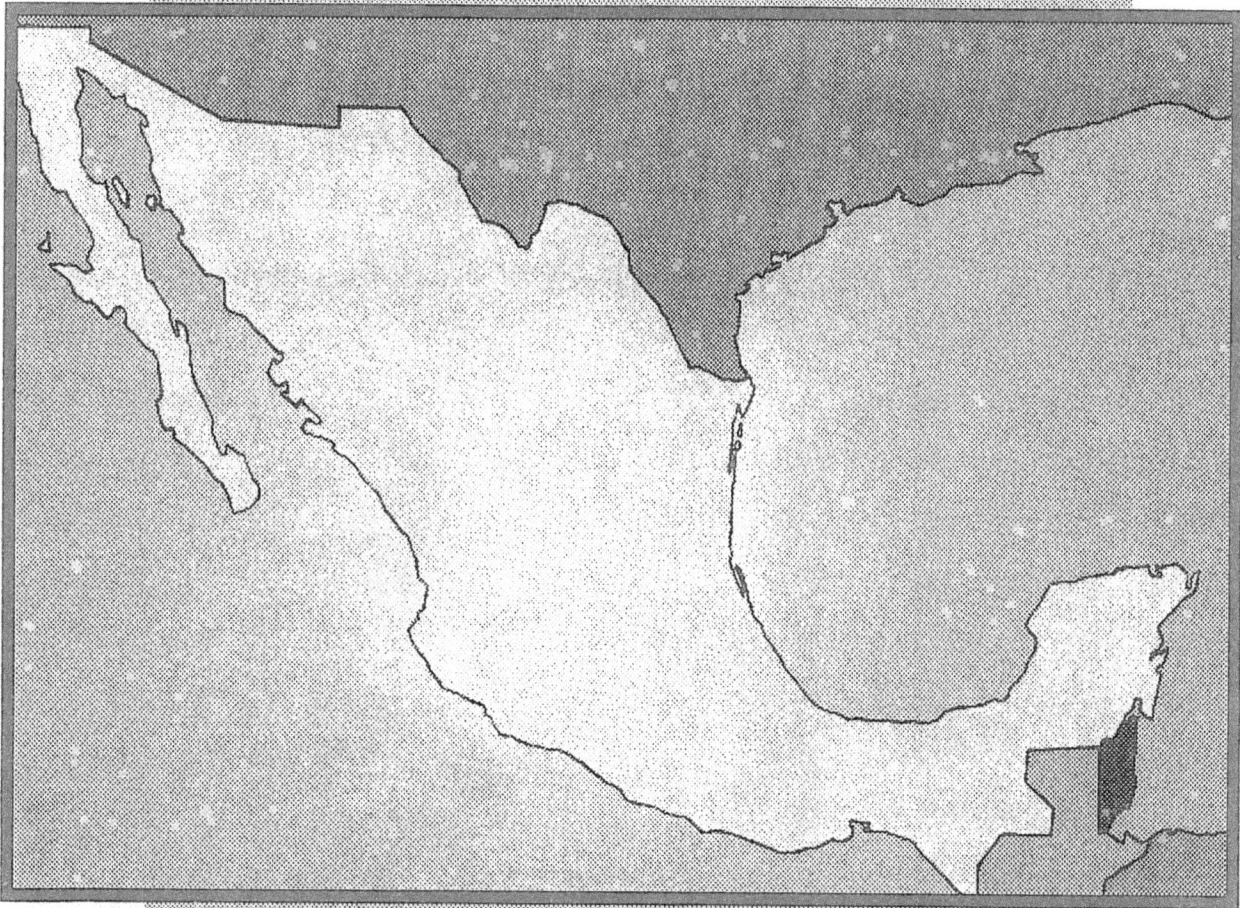

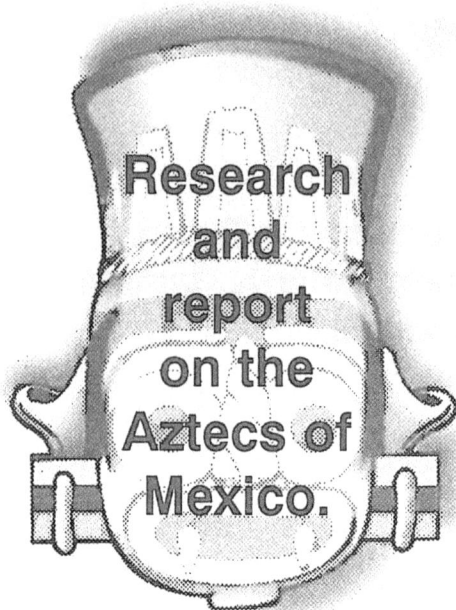

Research and report on the Aztecs of Mexico.

Create a menu of Mexican delights. Describe each food item.

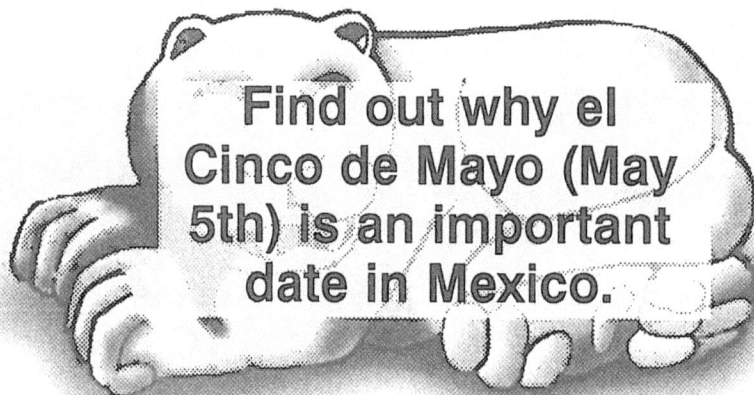

Find out why el Cinco de Mayo (May 5th) is an important date in Mexico.

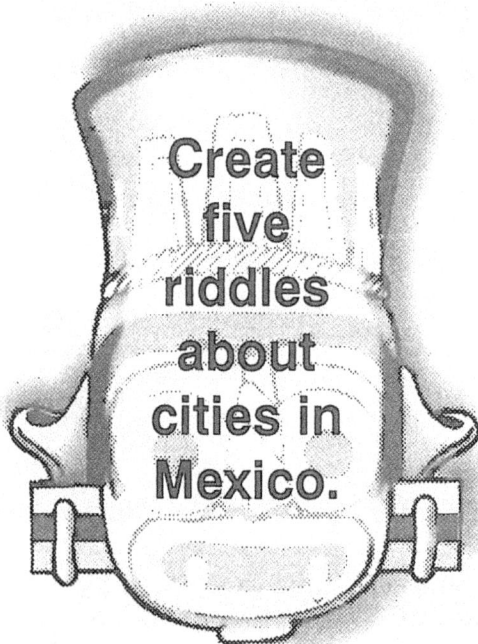

Create five riddles about cities in Mexico.

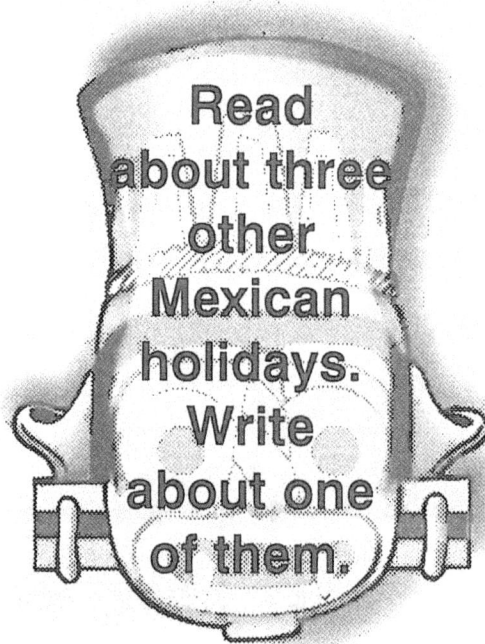

Read about three other Mexican holidays. Write about one of them.

What a Prize!

Independence Day in Mexico is celebrated with parades, floats, and fireworks! But that's not all! The celebration begins with one of the biggest events of all—the drawing of the winning number in the national lottery. It's worth millions.

Suppose you won the National Lottery and it was worth 3 million dollars. Brainstorm all things you might do with the money.

_____

_____

_____

_____

_____

_____

_____

_____

_____

_____

_____

_____

_____

_____

Citizenship Day

Citizenship Day is observed in the United States on September 17. This day was chosen because it was on September 17, 1787, that the final session of the Constitutional Convention was held. Thirty-nine delegates signed the Constitution before they left Philadelphia for their home states. Before the Constitution could become law in this land, however, at least nine of the original thirteen states would have to ratify, or approve, it.

A Good Citizen
List the obligations of a good citizen.

_____

_____

_____

_____

_____

_____

_____

_____

_____

_____

**What might you do to make yourself a better citizen?
Create a poster that shows what you might do!**

The U.S. Constitution

If you could add an amendment to the U.S Constitution, what would it be?

Find out what is meant by the Federalists. As a Federalist, write a letter to the editor of your newspaper.

Rank the 10 amendments known as the Bill of Rights in order of their importance to your life.

Find out why James Madison is called the Father of the Constitution.

As an Anti-Federalist try to convince a Federalist to change his or her mind.

The Twenty-Sixth Amendment

Create a political cartoon that illustrates the
change that occurred because of the Twenty-sixth Amendment.

Nathan Hale:
An American Patriot

It was September 1776, and things were going poorly for the Americans. General Washington was badly in need of information about the enemy's plans. Captain Nathan Hale volunteered to get that information; he would spy for General Washington!

Nathan, who had been a teacher before he joined the army, decided to pretend to be a loyalist schoolteacher looking for a job. He made his way behind enemy lines. Although untrained as a spy, he managed to obtain the information he was after. Unfortunately, he was captured by a British soldier before he could get back to safety.

Nathan had been caught red-handed. He was sentenced to death by hanging. On September 22, 1776—just before he died—he uttered his famous last words, "I regret that I have but one life to lose for my country." Little did he know that these words would be remembered for centuries to come.

"*I regret that I have but one life to lose for my country.*"

Join!

Create a recruitment poster for the Continental Army.

Heroes, Spies, and Patriots

What does it mean to be a patriot? Does Nathan Hale fit your description of a patriot?

The Americans and the British both used spies to obtain and transmit information about the other side. Research and write a report on Benedict Arnold.

What qualities does it take to be a spy?

What does it mean to be a hero? Does Nathan Hale fit your definition of a hero?

Create a booklet entitled Heroes and Heroines of the American Revolution.

Chinese Festival of the Autumn Moon

The Festival of the Autumn Moon takes place in September. It is held during the full moon in the eighth month of the Chinese lunar calendar. The festival begins with a procession in which lanterns in the shape of an animal, bird, or fish are carried. Following the procession is a feast with traditional foods like crabmeat and little rice cakes, which symbolize the full moon. The people ask the moon, whom they call Queen of Heaven, for good luck in the coming months.

Long ago, in the fourteenth century, when the Chinese rebelled against the Mongol leaders, rice cakes played an important role in the rebellion. See if you can figure out what the role was by solving this puzzle.

A. Written or spoken communications   _ _ S _ _ G _ _

B. A preposition   _ _ T H

C. Definite article   _ _ E

D. Hour and minute of a day (for example)   _ I _ _

E. A conjunction   _ N _

F. A location   _ _ A _ _

G. A preposition   _ F

H. Definite article   T _ _

I. Uprising   R _ _ _ _ _ _ _ N

J. Form of verb *to be* (past tense)   _ _ R _

K. Concealed   H _ _ _ _ _

L. A preposition   _ N

M. Definite article   _ H _

N. A cereal grass   R _ _ _

O. Sweet, baked mixture in loaf forms   _ A _ _ _

Rosh Hashanah & Yom Kippur

Rosh Hashanah is the Jewish New Year. It starts on the first day of the Hebrew month of *Tishri*. Usually, Rosh Hashanah falls in September, but sometimes it comes in October. Ten days later is *Yom Kippur*, the Day of Atonement. Yom Kippur is the most solemn day of the year for the Jewish people. On that day the people fast and pray for forgiveness for their sins.

An important theme of *Rosh Hashanah* and *Yom Kippur* is judgment. Jews examine their own acts and thoughts; they pray for forgiveness for their wrongdoings and promise not to repeat them.

SYMBOLS OF ROSH HASHANAH

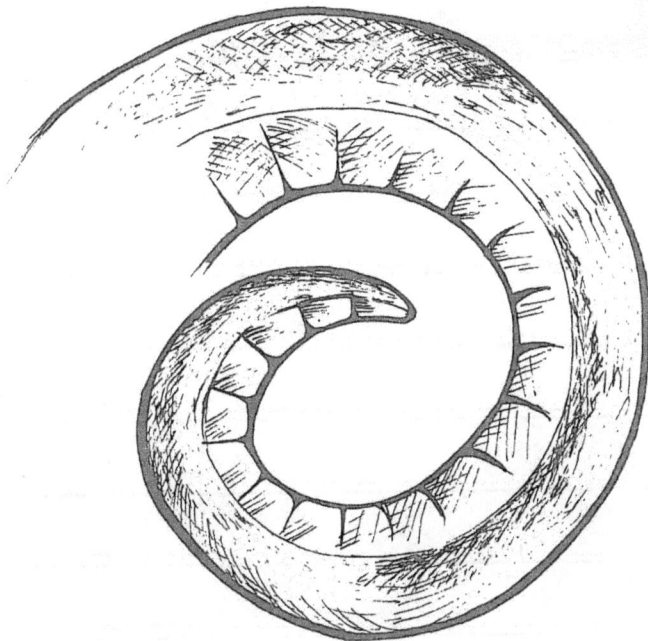

The *shofar,* or ram's horn, is the most important symbol. It is blown on Rosh Hashanah to announce the new year. It is blown again at the end of Yom Kippur to end the fast.

Honey is an important part of the Rosh Hashanah observance. People hope for a sweet year ahead. Honey is the symbol of that sweetness. Often, it is dripped on apples.

73

A Delicate Balance

The month of *Tishri* is Libra on the Zodiac. The Libra sign is a balance scale. Review all of your dealings with people over the last year. Classify your deeds into good or bad.

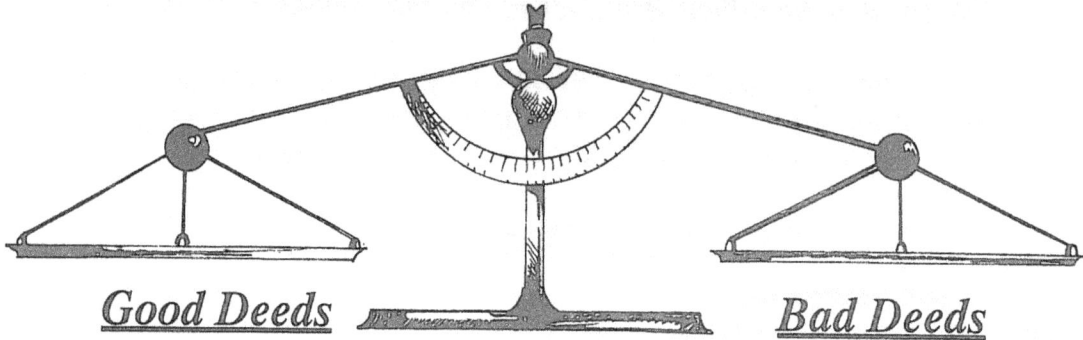

Good Deeds   *Bad Deeds*

_____   _____

_____   _____

_____   _____

_____   _____

_____   _____

_____   _____

_____   _____

_____   _____

Draw a balance scale that shows
how your good deeds compare with your bad deeds.

The Hebrew Calendar

There are twelve months in the Hebrew Calendar. A thirteenth month is added when it is a leap year. Although the new year begins with *Tishri,* preparation for the new religious year begins the previous month, *Elul.*

Elul (August/September)
Tishri (September/October)
Heshvan (October/November)
Kislev (November/December)
Tevet (December/January)
Shevat (January/February)
Adar (February/March)
Nisan (March/April)
Iyar (April/May)
Sevan (May/June)
Tammuz (June/July)
Av (July/August)

Eight Hebrew months are hidden in the following sentences.
See if you can find them.

1. Ann is an avid reader.

2. That, Eve thought, was a silly idea.

3. The glass had a whitish rim.

4. A darling little child came up to me.

5. Anne lulled the baby to sleep in the rocker.

6. His mom watched as Evan crossed the street.

7. The sink is level with the counter.

Create 3 hidden-word sentences using the months of the Gregorian calendar or the days of the week. Exchange with a classmate to solve.

_____

_____

_____

An Autumn Poem

Autumn begins with September 22 or 23. The following poem about autumn was written by American poetess Emily Dickinson. She lived from 1830 to 1886. It is written in quatrains, or four-lined poems.

Autumn

The morns are meeker than they were,
The nuts are getting brown;
The berry's cheek is plumper,
The rose is out of town.

The maple wears a gayer scarf,
The field a scarlet gown.
Lest I should be old-fashioned,
I'll put a trinket on.

Create one or more quatrains about Autumn.

_____

_____

_____

_____

_____

_____

_____

_____

_____

A Literature Unit

Johnny Appleseed

retold by Steven Kellogg

John Chapman, better known as Johnny Appleseed,
was born on September 26, 1774.
In honor of his birthday,
read *Johnny Appleseed*, retold by Steven Kellogg.

Johnny Appleseed

retold by Steven Kellogg

Story Summary:

John Chapman, later known as Johnny Appleseed, was born on September 24, 1774, in Leominster, Massachusetts. As soon as he was old enough, he left home and headed west. He took with him a bundle of apple seeds. It was his idea to clear land and plant orchards so that he could sell apple trees to the pioneer families as they settled their new lands.

John planted his first orchard in Franklin, Pennsylvania. He soon moved to Ohio; he planted orchards throughout the state. When Ohio became too crowded, he moved to Indiana. Often, John gave away his trees to families who needed his help. People started to call him Johnny Appleseed.

As time went on, legends about Johnny Appleseed grew. People talked about his adventures in the wilderness. Johnny Appleseed continued to clear land and plant orchards until he was just over 70. In March of 1845, however, he became ill while trudging through a snowstorm. He took refuge in a settler's cabin, but he died a few days later. Even after his death, legends about him persisted.

Comprehension & Discussion Questions
Based on Bloom's Taxonomy

Knowledge

1. What was Johnny Appleseed's real name?
2. Locate on a map the birthplace of John Chapman.
3. What season was it when Johnny Chapman was born?

Comprehension

4. Describe Johnny's attitude toward wildlife.
5. Johnny showed his cleverness when dealing with the woodman's challenge. Explain.
6. Explain what is meant by a lean-to.

Application

7. Find out a legend about Johnny Appleseed that was not described in the book. Write about it.
8. Create an apple cookbook.
9. Dramatize Johnny Appleseed's achievements.

Analysis

10. Read another tall tale. Compare and contrast it to *Johnny Appleseed.*
11. Analyze the importance of the orchards to the settlers.
12. Read another book about Johnny Appleseed. Compare and contrast it to Steven Kellogg's version.

Synthesis

13. Create a legend about Johnny Appleseed.
14. Write an acrostic poem about Johnny Appleseed.
15. Make up riddles about well-known folk heroes or heroines.

Evaluation

16. Judge the fact that Johnny Appleseed warned the settlers about Indian attacks.
17. Decide whether or not John Chapman was a generous man.
18. Predict what Johnny Appleseed would have done with his life had he been born in the 20th century.

Create a booklet describing how to make apple butter.

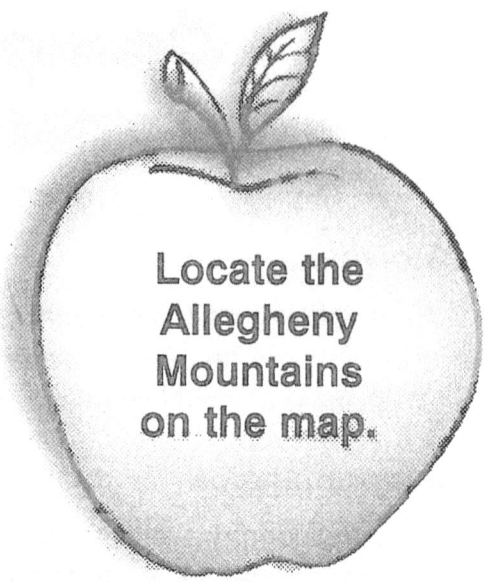

Locate the Allegheny Mountains on the map.

Under adult supervision make applesauce.

Map the journey of John Chapman.

Create a skit about Johnny Appleseed.

Brainstorm all the possible things you could do with apples. Stretch your imagination and include some unusual ideas.

Create a concrete (shape) poem about Johnny Appleseed.

Create an advertisement to encourage a book store to sell this book.

Create a Crossword Puzzle about *Johnny Appleseed.*

List many different kinds of fruits as you can. Classify them into groups. You must have at least two to a group. Use your Imagination.

Write five questions you would like to ask Johnny Appleseed.

Create a character sketch of Johnny Appleseed.

Create a picture cube about frontier life.

Create a song about Johnny Appleseed.

Create an annotated bibliography of folk tales.

Create an original tall tale.

_____

_____

_____

_____

_____

_____

_____

_____

_____

_____

_____

_____

_____

_____

_____

_____

_____

_____

_____

_____

_____

American Indian Day

American Indian Day is celebrated on the fourth Friday in September. By the time the Europeans arrived in America, Native Americans had already spread throughout North America. They developed a variety of cultures. Those cultures differed because the natural resources of their environments differed. The differences are evident in their homes, clothing, food supplies, tools and weapons, arts and crafts, and beliefs.

Cultural Areas

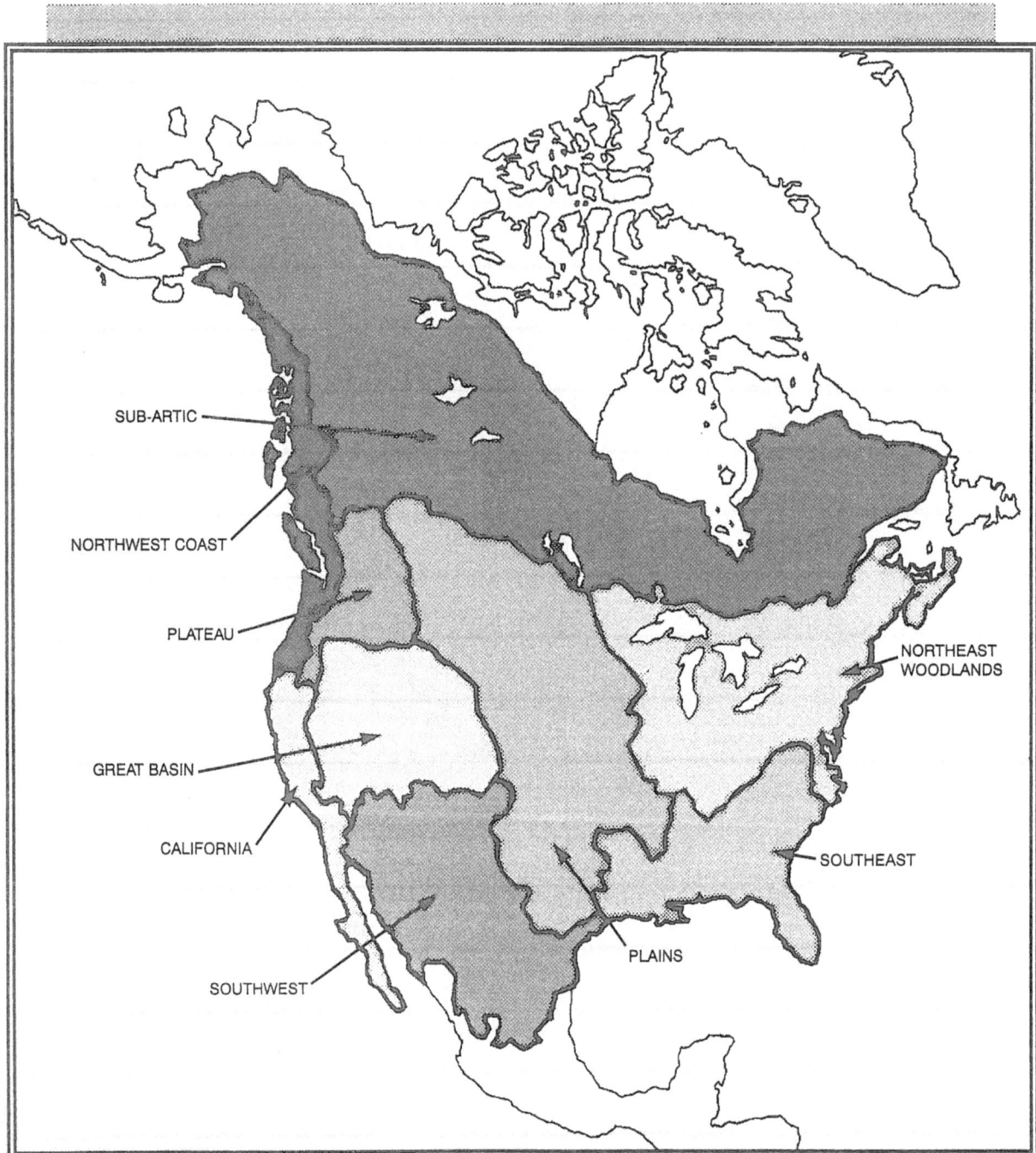

SUB-ARTIC

NORTHWEST COAST

PLATEAU

GREAT BASIN

CALIFORNIA

SOUTHWEST

PLAINS

NORTHEAST WOODLANDS

SOUTHEAST

Analyze the importance of the buffalo to the Plains Indians.

Create a fact file about the Creek Confederacy of the Southeast. Include at least six facts.

Research the Algonquin Indians of the Eastern Woodlands. Create a diorama that depicts their lifestyle.

Create a chart that shows the importance of forests and the seas to the culture of the people of the Northwest Coast.

Compare and contrast the lifestyle of the Navajos to that of the Pueblos.

Research the Iroquois of the Eastern Woodlands. Draw a picture that shows what is meant by the Three Sisters.

The Trail of Tears

The Indian Removal Act was passed in 1830. It established Indian Territory, now the state of Oklahoma. This land was chosen because it seemed unsuitable for the needs of the white settlers. The act also gave the U.S. government the ability to obtain land held by the Indians in exchange for land in the new Indian Territory.

Some tribes peacefully agreed to this resettlement. In the Southeast, however, things were different. The Cherokee, Chickasaw, Choctaw, Creek, and Seminole tribes had permanent homes and farms. Many had trades other than farming; some had complex systems of government. These Five Civilized Tribes, as they were called, did not want to give up their homes and farms for strange lands.

Although force was not called for in the original act, eventually it was used. About 100,000 people were forced to march across the country to Indian Territory. About 25 percent died along the way. The Cherokee call this terrible trek of 1838-39 the "Trail of Tears."

A Soliloquy

A *soliloquy* is a speech in which a character reveals his thoughts in the form of a monologue. Pretend that you are one of the Cherokees being forced to leave your home and march across the country. Write a soliloquy that reveals the way you feel as you are trekking across the country.

_____
_____
_____
_____
_____
_____
_____
_____
_____
_____
_____
_____
_____
_____

Famous Native Americans

___ 1. *Osceola*

___ 2. *Sequoya*

___ 3. *Chief Joseph*

___ 4. *Sacajawea*

___ 5. *Tecumseh*

___ 6. *Pontiac*

___ 7. *Massasoit*

___ 8. *Black Hawk*

___ 9. *John Ross*

___ 10. *Sitting Bull*

___ 11. *Red Cloud*

___ 12. *King Philip*

___ 13. *Samoset*

___ 14. *Geronimo*

___ 15. *Pocahontas*

___ 16. *Jim Thorpe*

A. Shawnee leader who tried to unite Western tribes

B. Sauk and Fox leader who defied the order to vacate tribal lands

C. Led Wampanoags in the severest war in New England history

D. Led Seminoles in Second Seminole War; resisted U.S. attempt to relocate

E. Selected by U.S. sports writers as greatest athlete of the first half of the 20th century

F. Wampanoag chief who kept peace with Pilgrims and shared useful knowledge

G. Created an alphabet and system of writing for the Cherokees

H. United Sioux tribes in their struggle for survival

I. Served as guide for Lewis and Clark Expedition

J. Cherokee leader who resisted removal but then led his people during the trek

K. Pemaquid Indian who befriended the Pilgrims

L. Nez Percé leader; conducted skilled but unsuccessful retreat from U.S. forces

M. Ottawa chief, organized intertribal resistance to British in the Great Lakes area

N. Her marriage to John Rolfe brought peace between the Powhatans and whites for a time

O. Chiracahua Apache; leader resisted white colonization of Southwest

P. Ogala (Sioux) chief; resisted U.S. attempt to develop a trail to gold mines in the Montana territory

Choose one of the Native Americans listed above and write a report.

Native American Legacy

List some foods that originated with Indians of North, Central, and South America.

N	A	T	I	V	E	N	Y	E	N	A
Q	L	I	R	Y	K	B	V	C	X	Z
E	N	N	N	T	R	I	B	E	S	N
N	E	N	W	O	R	D	N	P	F	U
N	I	A	M	E	R	I	C	A	N	W
A	F	L	I	S	O	N	Y	J	T	G

Create a word search of Native American tribes.

Read a Native American myth. Draw a series of pictures to tell the story.

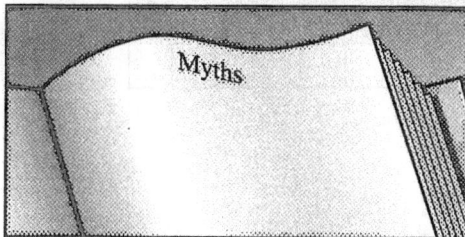

Myths

Compile a list of states which come from Native American words.

Construct a model of a totem pole.

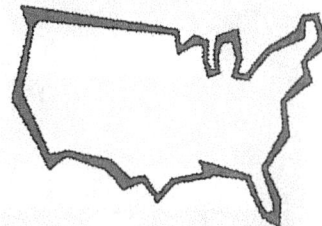

Spaniards brought horses to the New World. Analyze how this changed life for the Plains Indians.

September Crossword

ACROSS:

1. Wrote the *Star-Spangled Banner.*
6. Where the First Continental Congress met.
7. What the 13th amendment abolished.
8. Present state in location of Indian Territory.
10. What Agatha Christie wrote.
12. What Grandma Moses was.
13. Mexican-American labor leader.
15. Helped organize and discipline the troops at Vally Forge.
18. Spied for General Washington.
19. Olympic track-and-field specialist.
21. Season at end of September.
22. Unit of money in Mexico.
23. Author of *The War With Grandpa.*

DOWN:

2. The Cherokee call their trek of 1838-1839 the Trail of _____.
3. Founder of Hull-House.
4. Celebrated to honor workers.
5. Frenchman who helped Americans during American Revolution.
9. Traditional food of Festival of the Autumn Moon.
11. Father Miguel _____ is known as the father of the Mexican Revolution.
14. What Johnny Appleseed planted.
16. Sequoya invented the Cherokee _____.
17. Rosh Hashana is the Jewish _____.
20. Season at start of September.

September
Clip Art

SEPTEMBER

SUNDAY	MONDAY	TUESDAY	WEDNESDAY	THURSDAY	FRIDAY	SATURDAY

93

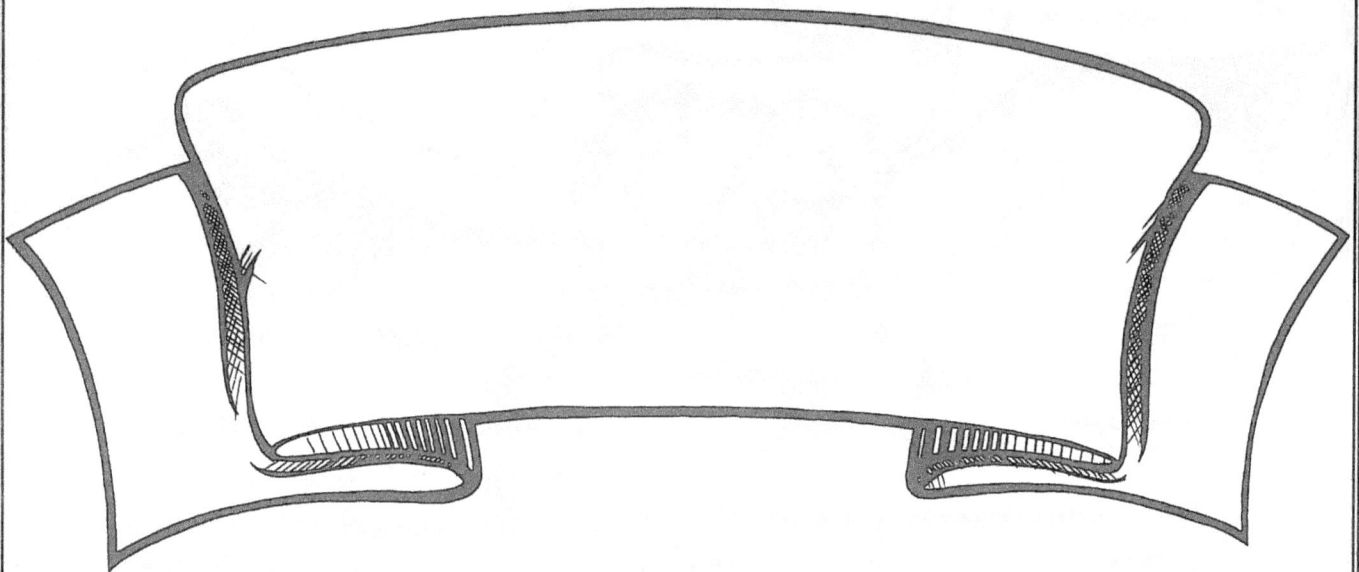

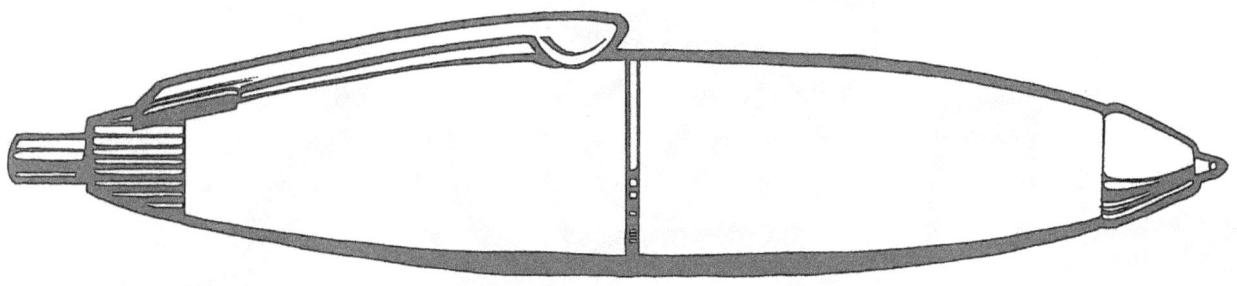

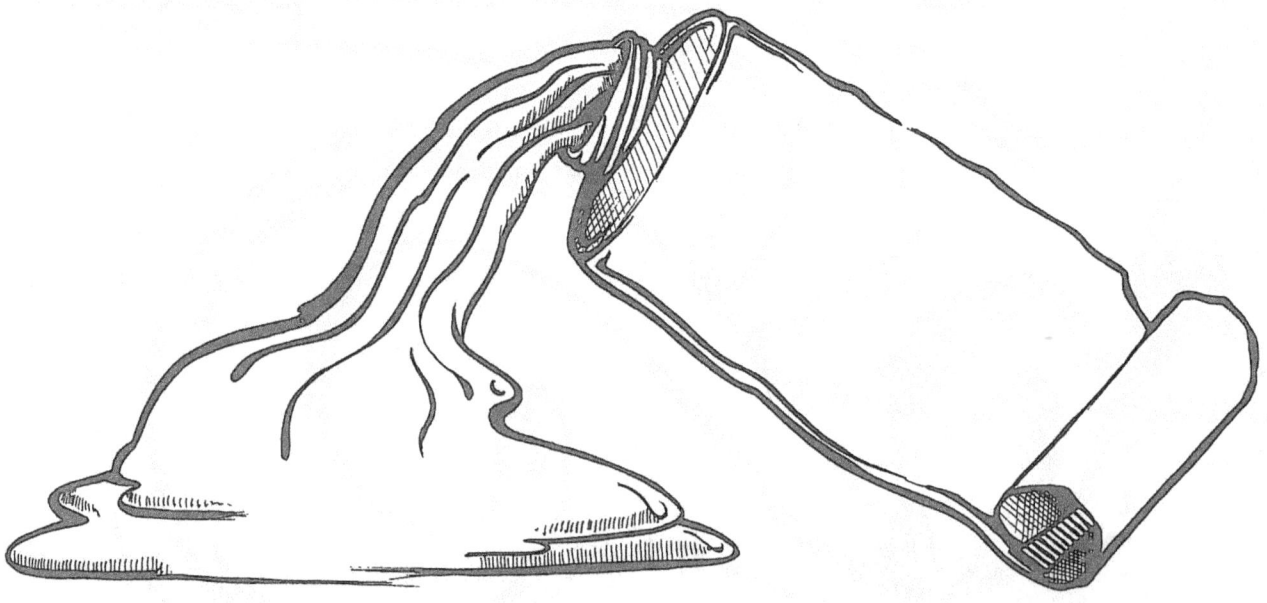

94

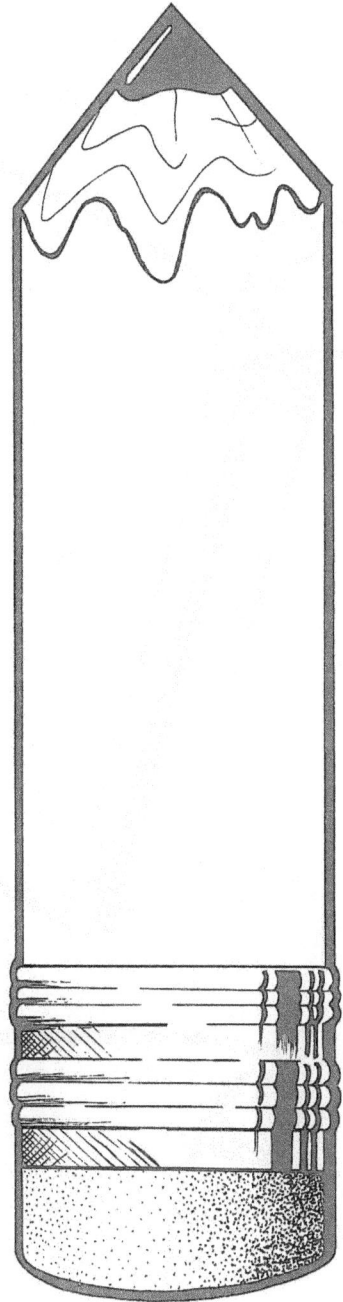
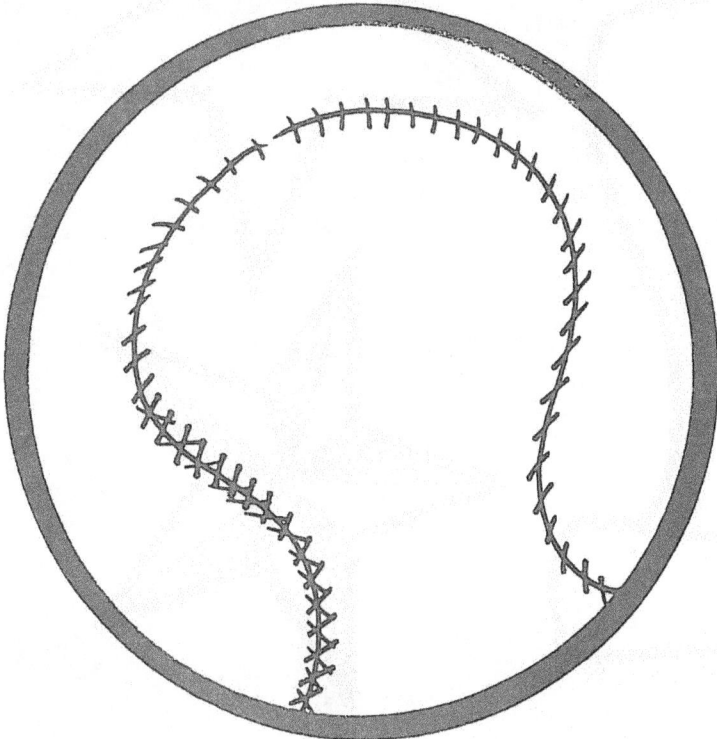

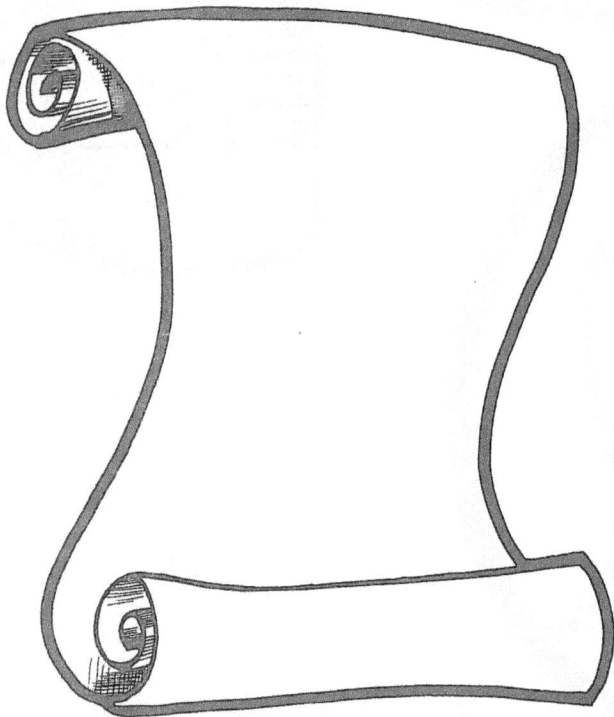

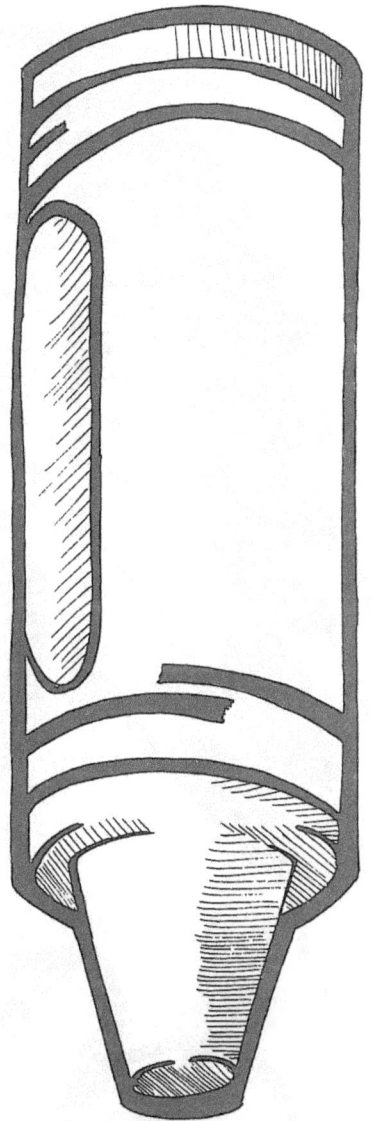

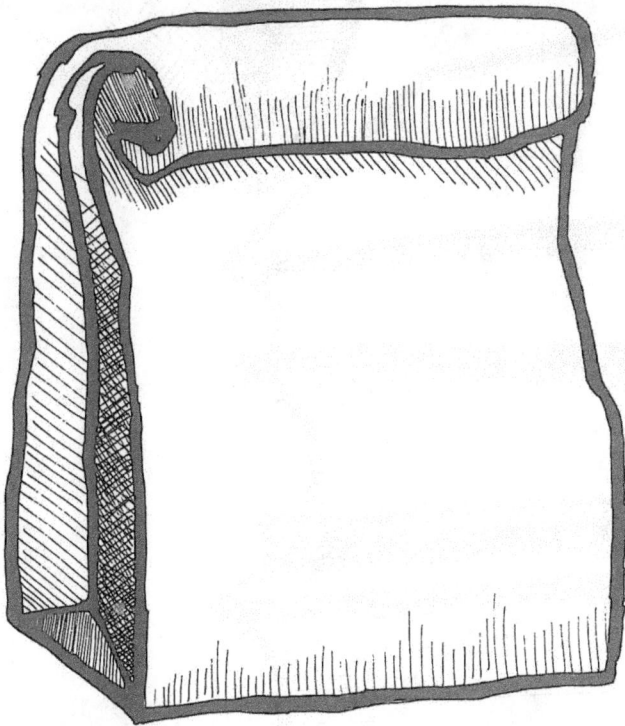

Bibliography

Bishop, Claire Huchet. *Lafayette.* Champaign, Illinois: Garrard Publishing Company, 1960.

Burnett, Bernice. *The First Book of Holidays, revised edition.* New York: Franklin Watts, Inc. 1974.

Chaikin, Miriam. *Sound the Shofar.* New York.: Clarion Books, 1986.

Fishwich, Marshall W. *Illustrious Americans: Jane Addams.* Morristown, New Jersey: Silver Burdett Company, 1968.

Graves, Charles P. *Grandma Moses, Favorite Painter.* Champaign, Illinois: Garrard Publishing Company, 1969.

Hogrogian, Robert. *Nathan Hale.* Hawthorne, New Jersey: January Productions, Inc., 1979.

Kellogg, Steven. *Johnny Appleseed.* New York: William Morrow and Company, Inc., 1988.

Marcus, Rebecca B. and Judith Marcus. *Fiesta Time in Mexico.* Champaign, Illinois: Garrard Publishing Company, 1974.

Owens, Jesse with Paul G. Neimark. *The Jesse Owens Story.* New York: G.P. Putnam's Sons, 1970.

Patterson, Lillie. *Francis Scott Key.* Champaign, Illinois: Garrard Publishing Company, 1963.

Rosen, Mike. *Autumn Festivals.* New York: The Bookright Press, 1990.

Smith, Robert Kimmel. *The War with Grandpa.* New York: Delacorte Press, 1984.

Stark, Rebbeca. *Native American Cultures.* Hawthorne, New Jersey: Educational Impressions, 1993.

Answers and Background information

Background information and answers are given as appropriate. Many activities call for original, creative answers. Answers are not given for those.

(Not Just) Openers: (pages 5-12)

Sept. 1: The 13th Amendment abolished slavery.

Sept. 2: Eugene Field wrote "Wynken, Blynken, and Nod" and "Little Boy Blue."

Sept. 3: Sullivan was one of the first to design a skyscraper with iron frames and straight lines. He's credited with inventing the skyscraper.

Sept. 4: George Eastman received a patent for his "Kodak" roll camera.

Sept. 5: Georgia did not send representatives.

Sept. 6: President McKinley was assassinated in Buffalo, New York, while attending the Pan-American Exposition.

Sept. 10: This secured the Northwest for the United States during the War of 1812.

Sept. 12: They discovered a prehistoric cave magnificently decorated with engraved, drawn, and painted animals. The cave is believed to have served as a center for the performance of hunting and magical rites.

Sept. 14: Sharecropping, or tenant farming, was a system of agricultural organization. The landowners contributed land; the tenants contributed labor. Each contributed varying amounts of capital and management. Payment to the landowners were in the form of a share of the crop, cash, or combination of both. Sharecropping became the accepted labor system throughout the South during the Reconstruction Period. The planters preferred it because they didn't have to pay wages. Without land or money, most freedmen had to continue working for their former masters. Now, however, they could live in individual cabins on tracts of land they rented. Sharecroppers found it very difficult to get out of debt; therefore, they were virtually bound to the soil, for the law prohibited them from leaving unless all their bills were paid. The South, however, was extremely poor during Reconstruction, and some bad crop years in the late 1860's followed by a general agricultural depression of the 1870's made matters worse.

Sept. 16: The *Mayflower* left Plymouth, England, with 102 passengers, including 32 children. There were 2 dogs and 25 crew members also on board. Rough seas and storms made their two-and-a-half-month journey in cramped conditions difficult to bear. The rough seas also kept them from reaching their planned destination, Virginia. Instead they landed at Provincetown, Massachusetts.

Sept. 17: Baron von Stuben helped train the troops at Valley Forge.

Sept. 18: Among the facts that might be included are the following: Washington was born on April 5, 1856, in Franklin County, Virginia. He was born in a slave hut. After emancipation, his family moved to West Virginia. As a child he worked in a salt furnace and a coal mine. He wanted an education; therefore, he got a job as a janitor to help pay expenses while attending the Hampton Normal and Agricultural Institute in Virginia. He returned to West Virginia and taught children at a day school and adults at night. He studied at Wayland Seminary in Washington, D.C., from 1878-79. In 1881, he headed the newly established Normal School for Blacks in Tuskegee. He became the institute's main developer. When he died on December 14, 1915, there were more than 100 buildings. Washington was the most influential spokesman for blacks between 1895 and 1915.

Sept. 19: *Steamboat Willie* was the first cartoon to use sound.

Sept. 20: Fiorello La Guardia was a U.S. Congressman and 3-term mayor of New York City (1933-35). He became known as the "Little Flower." La Guardia fought corruption, fostered civic improvement, and was pro-labor. He had a real flair for the dramatic. Once he assigned Jewish police officers to escort a visiting Nazi delegation. Another time he shut off the heat in the room where labor negotiations were being held to try to end a coal strike. He was also known for reading the Sunday comics over the radio to keep up morale.

Sept. 21: In 1673, Louis Joliet and Father Marquette traveled by canoe from Green Bay along the Fox, Wisconsin, and Mississippi Rivers. When they got to the mouth of the Arkansas River, they returned. They were certain that the Mississippi emptied into the Gulf of Mexico, not the Gulf of California as previously believed.

Sept. 23: He said, "I have not yet begun to fight."

Sept. 26: In March 1775, Daniel Boone and 28 others were hired to blaze a trail through the Cumberland Gap, a notch in the juncture of Virginia, Tennessee, and Kentucky. In spite of Indian attacks, they built the Wilderness Road. It ran from eastern Virginia to the interior of Kentucky. The road became the main route to the West. It made possible the opening of the first settlements in Kentucky.

Sept. 27: A caricature is a pictorial representation in which the subject's distinctive features or peculiarities are deliberately distorted or exaggerated.

Sept. 30: Roger Maris broke Babe Ruth's record in 1961. Both Ruth and Maris played for the New York Yankees.

Hidden Back-to-School Words (page 15)

1. bus   2. paper   3. bookmark   4. pen   5. teacher   6. ruler   7. play   8. student   9. homework   10. learn

The War with Grandpa (pages 24-32)

Chapters 1-5: Vocabulary: 1.c 2.e 3.d 4.f 5.a 6.b

Chapters 1-5: Comprehension and Discussion

1. Pete tells the story from his point of view. The word "I" refers to Pete.
2. A billboard is a structure used to display advertisements. Jennifer had things written on most of her clothes.
3. Jennifer found out that their grandfather was moving into Pete's room. She had overheard her mother's conversation. Although she didn't tell Pete that Grandpa was moving into his room, she did say that Pete would be moving into the guest room; this amounted to the same thing.
4. He was familiar with it.
5. Answers will vary.

Chapters 6-10: Vocabulary: 1.c 2.e 3.g 4.f 5.b 6.d 7.a

Chapters 6-10: Comprehension and Discussion

1. It shows that he understood that it is necessary for parents to enforce certain rules for their children's own benefit.
2. The main point is that Pete was afraid to sleep upstairs by himself.
3. Jenny said she loved Grandpa because he sent her candy on her birthday. Pete loved his grandparents because they enjoyed his company. Everything he did was O.K. with them.
4. His grandmother had emphysema, and the warm air was better for her lungs.
5. Grandpa was so sad that he seemed lifeless.

Chapters 11-16: Vocabulary: 1.c 2.f 3.a 4.e 5.g 6.b 7.d

Chapters 11-16: Comprehension and Discussion

1. Before Grandma's illness Grandpa was peppy and full of life. He loved to do things with Pete. After her death, he just moped around and did nothing.
2. "To egg on" means to encourage or incite to action. In this chapter Pete's friends "egged him on" and encouraged him to start a war with Grandpa to regain his room.
3. Answers will vary.
4. Answers will vary.

5. Answers will vary, but the chapter title might be the answer. It takes 2 sides to fight.

Chapters 17-21: Vocabulary: 1.c 2.e 3.f 4.a 5.b 6.d

Chapters 17-21: Comprehension and Discussion

1. Answers will vary.
2. A flag of truce, a white flag, signifies that the party flying it wants to put a temporary stop to the fighting to talk things over.
3. Answers will vary.
4. A pun is a play on words. Although "defeeted" is not a real word, Pete intentionally misspelled it because he was taking the slippers. Grandpa called Pete "a slippery customer." "Slippery" referred to the fact that he stole the slippers. "Slippery" means elusive or evasive.
5. Answers will vary, but it made it seem as if he wasn't taking him seriously.

Chapters 22-25: Vocabulary: 1.c 2.a 3.e 4.f 5.b 6.d

Chapters 22-25: Comprehension and Discussion

1. Answers will vary.
2. Answers will vary, but it probably upset him that Pete was comparing war to a game. Grandpa knew that people lose lives in a war, and he did not like it being thought of so casually.
3. A simile is the comparison of two unlike things using the words "like" or "as." Pete said, "She looks like a small stork or a large chicken, when she stands on one foot."
4. He stole the playing pieces, properties, and rules from Pete's Monopoly game.
5. It meant that he had entered the war.

Chapters 26-28: Vocabulary: 1.d 2.c 3.e 4.a 5.b 6.f

Chapters 26-28: Comprehension and Discussion

1. He said the Monopoly pieces were prisoners of war.
2. It made him interested in life once again. He fixed Pete's rocker, was determined to fix other things around the house, and regained his sense of humor.
3. High tide was at 9:07 A.M. Grandpa said that at high tide the water comes into the harbor and brings with it the food the fish like to eat. The fish, therefore, come to feed. They are more likely to take the bait.
4. He said the tide pulled him right out of bed at four-thirty in the morning. He was referring to the fact that because of the tide he had to get up so early.
5. Pete stole the watch that Grandma had given him.

Chapters 29-32: Vocabulary: 1.c 2.d 3.f 4.g 5.a 6.e 7.b

Chapters 29-32: Comprehension and Discussion

1. Pete knew that something was about to happen, but didn't know when.
2. Answers will vary, but he probably didn't want to get other family members involved.
3. He changed Pete's alarm so that Pete would have to rush; he hid his slippers, toothbrush, underwear, and socks; he turned his jeans inside out, hid his belt, and took the laces out of his sneakers; and he hid his books.
4. Because he had rushed, he forgot his lunch.
5. "War isn't such fun after all."

Chapters 33-37: Vocabulary: 1.e 2.d 3.g 4.a 5.f 6.b 7.c

Chapters 33-37: Comprehension and Discussion

1. Answers will vary.
2. Answers will vary, but Pete probably realized that he had humiliated him. Pete loved Grandpa and never intended to hurt him so deeply.
3. He learned that things can easily escalate and get out of hand. Each action causes a worse reaction from the other side.
4. They talked it over and decided to try to convince Dad to let Grandpa convert the basement, where his office was, into an apartment.
5. He learned that you have to decide for yourself what is wrong or right.

Chicago (page 40)

There had been a population explosion caused primarily by the large influx of immigrants. Added to this were the ex-farmers who had deserted the land after the depression of 1873. The different immigrant groups disliked each other because of old animosities. The city was riddled with violence and corruption.

Who was President? (page 43)

The following people were President during the lifetime of Grandma Moses:

1857-1861	James Buchanan	1897-1901	William McKinley
1861-1865	Abraham Lincoln	1901-1909	Theodore Roosevelt
1865-1869	Andrew Jackson	1909-1913	William Howard Taft
1869-1877	Ulysses S. Grant	1913-1921	Woodrow Wilson
1877-1881	Rutherford B. Hayes	1921-1923	Warren G. Harding
1881	James A. Garfield	1923-1929	Calvin Coolidge
1881-1885	Chester A. Arthur	1929-1933	Herbert Hoover
1885-1889	Grover Cleveland	1933-1945	Franklin Delano Roosevelt
1889-1893	Benjamin Harrison	1945-1953	Harry S. Truman
1893-1897	Grover Cleveland	1953-1961	Dwight D. Eisenhower

Extra: On April 14, 1865, Abraham Lincoln was assassinated by Confederate supporter John Wilkes Booth. President Garfield was shot on July 2, 1881, by Guiteau. He shot him because he wasn't given an appointment to a government job as expected.

Fact or Opinion (page 45)

1. F 2.F 3.F 4.O 5.O 6.O 7.F 8. O 9.F 10. O

The Pledge of Allegiance (page 46)

Possible answers are as follows:

1. pledge/promise
2. allegiance/loyalty
3. republic/a political order with a president
4. stands/represents
5. indivisible/not capable of being divided
6. liberty/freedom from unjust control
7. justice/moral rightness

The Star-Spangled Banner (page 50)

The missing words are dawn's, proudly, twilight's, stripes, ramparts, streaming, rocket's, bombs, proof, wave, free, and brave.

Hispanic Heritage Week (page 57)

1. H
2. O
3. G
4. A
5. F
6. D
7. K
8. I
9. M
10. L
11. N
12. P
13. B
14. E
15. C
16. J

Hablo Español (page 59)

1. Mexico
2. Cuba
3. Puerto Rico
4. Spain
5. Honduras
6. Argentina
7. Colombia
8. Peru
9. Costa Rica
10. Nicaragua

¿Cuántos dólares? (page 62)

1. $6.65
2. 80 cents
3. $4.66
4. $33.25

Mexico (page 63)

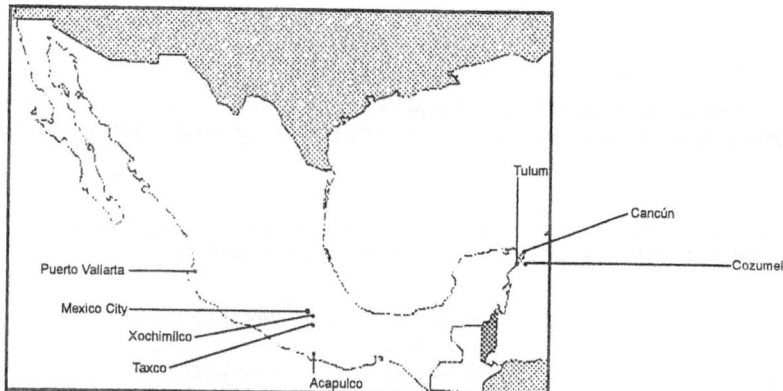

El Cinco de Mayo or May 5th (page 64)

El Cinco de Mayo, or May 5th, is an important Mexican holiday. On this date in 1862, after about four hours of fighting, about 4,000 Mexican soldiers defeated about 10,000 well-trained French ones. The French finally retreated.

The U.S. Constitution (page 67)

Federalists were advocates of the new Constitution; they favored ratification. Anti-Federalists were opposed to ratification.

James Madison is called the Father of the U.S. Constitution. He took careful, detailed notes of the debate. Madison's notes, which weren't published until a few years after his death, became our main source of information about the convention. He also suggested a plan for a system of checks and balances in which there would be three branches of government. He joined Alexander Hamilton and John Jay in their effort to persuade the states to ratify it; their essays were collected in the book called *The Federalists*.

The Twenty-Sixth Amendment (page 68)

This amendment lowered the voting age from 21 to 18.

Heroes, Spies, and Patriots (page 71)

Benedict Arnold was a loyal Patriot until he shifted allegiance to the British in 1779. His name became synonymous with *traitor*. He informed the British of a proposed American invasion of Canada.

Chinese Festival of the Autumn Moon (page 72)

Messages with the time and place of the rebellion were hidden in the rice cakes.

The Hebrew Calendar (page 75)

1. a. Nisan   b. Av   2. Tevet   3. Tishri   4. Adar   5. Elul   6. Sevan   7. Kislev

Johnny Appleseed (pages 77-83)

1. Johnny Appleseed's real name was John Chapman.
2. He was born in Leominster, Massachusetts.
3. He was born in autumn.
4. He loved animals and would not harm them.
5. He suggested they have a tree-chopping match rather than a wrestling match. In that way he got the land cleared for the next orchard.
6. A lean-to is a shelter having a roof with only one slope.
11. It would take a while for the settlers to build their farms. The young apple trees would have been welcome in these new lands.

Importance of Buffalo to the Plains Indians (page 85)

The buffalo provided for almost every need: The meat was their main food (some roasted, some dried and stored for the future, and some pounded with fat and berries for pemmican); the hides were used to make tepees, clothing, moccasins, robes, and blankets; and the bones, teeth, and horns were used to make tools and utensils.

Lifestyle of the Algonquins (page 85)

They lived in wigwams covered with animal skins and birchbark. They hunted deer, caribou, and other animals with bone and stone-tipped arrows. They used deadfalls and snares. Cooking pots and utensils were made from birchbark. They also made birchbark canoes. Fishing was a year-round activity. Men wore breechclouts and leggings; moccasins were soft soled. They also wore a headdress called an artificial roach. Women wore skirts, leggings, and sometimes a cape. They embroidered them with porcupine quills. They, too, wore soft-soled moccasins.

Iroquois: 3 Sisters (page 85)

The Iroquois were farmers. The Three Sisters were corn, beans, and squash.

Creek Confederacy Facts (page 85)

The Creek Confederacy was in the Southeastern U.S. They were part of the Muskhogean language family. Field of corn, squash, beans, and fruit surrounded the town. The Creek Confederacy was made up of about 50 tribes; towns were often stockaded. Men cleared the land. Women did most of the planting and harvesting. They were hunters as well as farmers. Cane was used to make blowguns and knives. A central square served as a public meeting place. Stickball was popular. Creek families, or clans, were split into two divisions: The Red (warriors) and the White (religious leaders and healers). Clubs and bows and arrows were important weapons. The Seminoles were at one time part of the Creek Confederacy.

Importance of the Forest to the Northwest Coast Indians (page 85)

The forest provided wood for plank houses, totem poles, dugout canoes, fishing hooks and spears, containers, and armor.

Navajos/Pueblos (page 85)

The Navajos learned a lot from the Pueblos but adapted what they learned to suit their needs. Pueblos lived in multi-dwelling pueblos. The Navajos lived in hogans. The Pueblos were farmers, and the Navajos learned to farm. The Pueblo men were weavers, and the Navajos learned to weave from them. Unlike the Pueblos, the Navajo women did the weaving. The Pueblo women wore cotton dresses. The Navajos abandoned buckskin clothes and adapted the Pueblo dress with some adaptations.

Famous Native Americans (page 88)

1. D	3. L	5. A	7. F	9. J	11. P	13. K	15. N
2. G	4. I	6. M	8. B	10. H	12. C	14. O	16. E

Foods That Originated with Indians of North, Central, and South America (page 89)

Some of the foods were avocado, sunflower seeds, maize (corn), squash, wild cherries, sweet potatoes, tomatoes, maple sugar, chocolate, and pumpkin.

Tribes for Word Search (page 89)

Haida, Tlingit, Yurok, Tsimshian, Navajo, Pueblo, Apache, Creek, Cherokee, Seminole, Chicasaw, Natchez, Pawnee, Mandan, Sioux, Cheyenne, Blackfoot, Choctaw, Algonquin, Iroquois, Kwakiutl, Zuni, Pomo, Paiute, and Nootka are a few suggestions.

States with Indian Names (page 89)

State	Meaning	State	Meaning
1. Alabama	reap the land	14. Missouri	muddy waters
2. Arizona	place of the little creek	15. Nebraska	river broad
3. Arkansas	land of the small creek	16. New Mexico	land of Mexitlt
4. Connecticut	long river	17. North Dakota	friend
5. Idaho	light on mountain	18. Ohio	beautiful water
6. Illinois	superior men; warrior	19. Oklahoma	red people
7. Iowa	one who puts to sleep	20. Oregon	land of the beaver
8. Kansas	plain	21. South Dakota	friend
9. Kentucky	meadow land	22. Tennessee	a Cherokee name (Tenassee)
10. Massachusetts	large hill place	23. Texas	ally
11. Michigan	land of the big lake	24. Utah	higher land
12. Minnesota	cloudy water	25. Wisconsin	gathering of waters
13. Mississippi	big river	26. Wyoming	large prairie place

What Horses Did for the Plains Indians (page 89)

From then on they could hunt the buffalo from horseback. The horse travois made it possible to transport larger tepees than with the dog travois. Most tribes gave up farming entirely to follow the great herds of buffalo.

Crossword Puzzle (page 90)

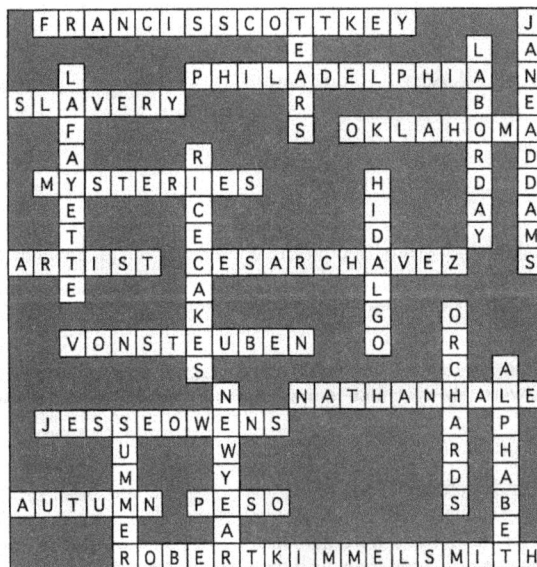